Benessere Psicologico

Contemporary Thought on Italian American Mental Health

Dominick Carielli and Joseph Grosso
EDITORS

JOHN D. CALANDRA ITALIAN AMERICAN INSTITUTE
QUEENS COLLEGE, CITY UNIVERSITY OF NEW YORK

STUDIES IN ITALIAN AMERICANA
VOLUME 7

John D. Calandra Italian American Institute
Queens College, CUNY
25 West 43rd Street, 17th floor
New York, NY 10036

ISBN 978-1-939323-00-2
Library of Congress Control Number: 2013952599

This book is dedicated to two former Calandra counselors who have passed away, Jeffrey A. F. Ballerini and Marianne DiPalermo McCauley. Both of these individuals were extremely passionate about, and dedicated to, their profession. They cared deeply about the people to whom they provided services and they were very proud of their Italian heritage. Although somewhat different in demeanor, Jeff a quiet and gentle soul and Marianne more of a fireball, they each brought joy to others in their own unique way. The spirit of each of these exceptional people lives on at the Calandra Institute through the good works of the counselors.

CONTENTS

PART THREE
THEORY AND TREATMENT

Foreword

Benessere Psicologico: Contemporary Thought on Italian American Mental Health appears in 2013 as a first of its kind. Over the years there has been much research done on Italian Americans from a variety of perspectives: From the sociological to the anthropological, from the literary to the cinematic, and a plethora of studies in history as well. Within the realm of psychology, however, the field has not been anywhere as fertile as in other fields. Indeed, one might even speak in terms of a dearth of research, for which the field remains wide open and ripe for cultivation of various discourses.

Thus, to date, the number of studies available on Italian American mental health, which is the phrase we have decided to use here, is small, to be sure;[1] the Italian part of the anthology's title, *benessere psicologico*, in fact, translates as "psychological wellbeing." The one psychological study that dates back to World War II is Irvin Child's *Italian or American? The Second Generation in Conflict*.[2] As far as any bibliographical search might reveal, this is the first book-length study on, as he entitled his second chapter, the "psychological significance of the social situation." It deals with three different types of "reactions" that may very well inform the second-generation Italian as he or she reacts to his or her experience in moving from an immigrant environment at home to a more "American" milieu outside the home at school and at work. We have the "rebel reaction" which pushes the Italian to a decidedly American way of life; the "in-group reaction" which results in the individual remaining well ensconced in his or her immigrant milieu; and the "apathetic reaction" by which the individual tries to negotiate, and thus reconcile, the two worlds he or she inhabits.

---

[1] One might indeed argue here for the inclusion of the likes of Paul Campisi, Herbert Gans, Joseph Lopreato, and Phyllis Williams, just to mention four names that inhabit more the sociological world of research on Italian Americans. I would not include them here for the very reason that they are predominantly sociological in nature, whereas those studies I mention in these opening remarks are squarely psychological.

[2] This is a result of his Ph.D. dissertation at Yale University, which he finished in 1938. His subjects were part of the Italian community in New Haven, Connecticut.

It is not until the 1980s that we find substantial essays on Italian Americans and mental health, notably Joseph Giordano's co-authored 1982 essay "Italian Families." Giordano had preceded this essay with some other work, basically his 1975 paper "An Italian-American Identity: A Positive Perspective" and his subsequent co-authored working paper *Mental Health and Middle America: A Group Identity Approach*, published in pamphlet form. This work was followed by another innovative approach authored by Aileen Riotto Sirey, Lisa Mann, and Anthony Patti: *Ethnotherapy: An Exploration of Italian-American Identity*. In the first decade of this century, two significant pieces occur. In 2001, Donna Chirico explored the psychological implications of the Roman Catholic Church in the United States on Italian Americans and, in so doing, posed difficulties in studying Italian Americans. In an analogous fashion, Elizabeth Messina discussed the detrimental effects stereotypes can have on younger Italian Americans, especially when they are "perpetuated by dominant social institutions" through such popular shows as *The Sopranos*.[3]

All of this is what subtends the symposium from which this book was born. As a result, we come to realize that we are still in a somewhat nascent state of research vis-à-vis a national discourse on Italian-American mental health. This book constitutes a major initial step in solidifying that discourse, as it now figures as part of a foundational collective poised to take the conversation to yet another level.

Benessere Psicologico: Contemporary Thought on Italian American Mental Health is part of a greater research initiative at the John D. Calandra Italian American Institute that has its roots in the founding of such series as *Studies in Italian Americana* and *Transactions*, and the books published herein. If we do not engage, in both a rigorous and substantial manner, in those national conversations on these and other issues, we shall never be part of the national dialogue and hence not benefit from such discussions. That said, both Dominick Carielli and Joseph Grosso join others here at the Calandra Institute in developing further our overall contribution to the intellectual community of Italian America.

ANTHONY JULIAN TAMBURRI
John D. Calandra Italian American Institute

---

[3] Of a more popular nature and falling under the umbrella of "self-help" are two books by Raeleen D'Agostino Mautner: *Living La Dolce Vita* and *Lemons into Limoncello*.

References

Campisi, Paul. 1948. "Ethnic Family Patterns: The Italian Family in the United States." *The American Journal of Sociology* 53.6: 443-49.

Child, Irvin L. 1943. *Italian or American? The Second Generation in Conflict.* New Haven, CT: Yale University Press.

Chirico, Donna. 2001. "Exoteric and Esoteric Imagination in Psychological Development," *Social Compass* 48.4: 525-39.

Gans, Herbert J. 1962. *Urban Villagers: Group and Class in the Life of Italian-Americans.* New York: The Free Press.

Giordano, Joe, Monica McGoldrick, and Joanne Guarino Klages. 1996. "Italian Families." In *Ethnicity and Family Therapy,* 2nd ed., edited by Monica McGoldrick, Joe Giordano, and John K. Pearce, 567–82. New York: Guilford.

Giordano, Joseph and Grace Pineiro Giordano. 1977. *The Ethno-Cultural Factor in Mental Health: Literature Review and Bibliography.* New York: Institute on Pluralism and Group Identity of the American Jewish Committee.

_____, and Marion Levine. 1975. *Mental Health and Middle America: A Group Identity Approach.* New York: Institute on Pluralism and Group Identity.

_____. 1975. "An Italian-American Identity: A Positive Perspective," paper presented at the American Italian Historical Association. Flushing, NY.

Lopreato, Joseph. 1970. *Italian Americans.* New York: Random House.

Mautner, Raeleen D'Agostino. 2013. *Lemons into Limoncello: From Loss to Personal Renaissance with the Zest of Italy.* Deerfield Beach, FL: Health Communications, Inc.

_____. 2003. *Living La Dolce Vita: Bring the Passion, Laughter and Serenity of Italy into Your Daily Life.* Naperville, IL: Sourcebooks.

Messina, Elizabeth G. 2004. "Psychological Perspectives on the Stigmatization of Italian Americans in the Media." In *Saints and Rogues: Conflicts and Convergence in Psychotherapy,* edited by Robert Marchesani and E. Mark Sterns. New York: The Haworth Press. 87-121.

_____. 1994. "Life-span development and Italian American Women." In *Italian Americans in a Multicultural Society,* edited by Jerome Krase and Judith DeSena. Stonybrook, NY: Forum Italicum.

Sirey, Aileen Riotto, Lisa Mann, and Anthony Patti. 1985. *Ethnotherapy: An Exploration of Italian-American Identity.* National Institute for the Psychotherapies.

Williams, Phyllis H. 1938. *South Italian Folkways in Europe and America: A Handbook for Social Workers, Visiting Nurses, School Teachers, and Physicians.* New Haven, CT: Yale University Press.

Preface

"Mental health problems do not affect three or four out of every five persons, but one out of one."
— William C. Menninger

The above quotation has always held a special place in my heart since I first read it many years ago. In fact, I still keep a copy of it, printed on a scrap of paper, in my briefcase. I cannot tell you from which publication it was clipped, but I can tell you that Dr. Menninger's assertion is true. Certainly, all of us, at many points in our lives, experience mental health issues. Beyond that, we are often affected by the emotional and psychological problems of those who are close to us.

Since 1979, the counselors of the Calandra Institute (then, the Italian American Institute to Foster Higher Education) have been addressing the mental health needs of Italian Americans, who, along with many other white ethnic groups, were largely left out of the multicultural counseling movement that was taking hold during that era. The prevailing belief was that all western Europeans were a homogeneous group and, thus, the particular mental health needs of Italian Americans were not addressed. This led to a dearth of research and discourse on Italian American mental health that has persisted to the present time. *Benessere Psicologico* is an attempt to fill some of that void.

This book is divided into three parts, and each section has a particular focus. Part I examines culture and identity. I cannot think of a topic that is more critical to a volume dedicated to mental health in the Italian American community. From their early immigration to this country, Italian Americans have had a muddled racial and ethnic identity. They have also faced discrimination and ethnic stereotyping by the media.

In the first essay, Richard Gambino looks at the enduring legacy of media stereotyping and defamation of Italian Americans. He views such stereotyping in the popular media as a virtual depiction of Italian American culture; one that is in conflict with the cultural reality that is personally experienced by Italian Americans. He posits that such conflict can lead to anxiety and identity confusion, potentially resulting in a myriad of psychological problems that can include self-limiting and self-defeating thoughts and behaviors.

In the next essay, Donna Chirico examines identity development among Italian American youth, issues of whiteness versus nonwhiteness, and the relatively poor educational attainment of Americans of Italian descent. She proposes that the development of a transcendent imagination, which she sees as essential for mental health and wellness, allows individuals to surmount barriers created by ethnic traditions, which can limit options and opportunities.

Part I concludes with an empirical study that explores cultural identity and the sense of home and belonging among post World War II Italian Immigrants. Using questionnaires and in-person interviews, Lucia Imbesi investigates the experience of leaving one's home and the effects that a new environment has on cultural identity. She delves into issues of how these immigrants view themselves, the adjustments that they make, and the resolution of any cultural conflicts that they have been experiencing.

Part II is a very unique contribution to the field of Italian American mental health. In these essays, three individual discuss their personal experiences with mental health issues and the treatment they received. Seeing a mental health practitioner has always carried with it a certain stigma. Although much has changed during the last few decades regarding attitudes toward seeking professional psychological help, this stigma still exists. This may be particularly true for Italian Americans, who have had a reluctance to discuss personal matters with strangers, and who generally do not go outside the family for help. The authors of these essays are to be commended for their willingness to share their personal struggles with us. I'm sure that their stories will provide valuable insights and information for therapists working with Italian Americans and for those potential clients who may wish to obtain psychological services for themselves.

First, Christina Bruni candidly discusses her mental breakdown at age twenty-two, her hospitalization, and her subsequent diagnosis of schizophrenia. She takes us on a journey from that initial breakdown to her recovery, and to her eventually becoming a librarian and an outspoken activist for mental health issues. Interspersed throughout the essay are

Bruni's suggestions for anyone who may be living with a mental illness, along with references to several websites. Her story is inspirational, and may be especially helpful to anyone trying to cope with a severe and chronic mental illness.

Next, Gil Fagiani talks about his experiences in a therapeutic community (TC), where he received treatment for drug addiction. Fagiani looks back at his experiences not solely as a client, but also as a mental health professional who has treated people with substance abuse, and who had directed a TC for twenty years. During the 1960s and 1970s, there was a great deal of innovation and experimentation in the counseling field with regard to treatment modalities. The treatment of substance abuse was certainly no exception, and epitomizes much of what occurred during those tumultuous times. Fagiani gives us a rare glimpse inside the often bizarre world of substance abuse treatment, whose methods would seem strange, perhaps even unethical, by today's standards.

Finally, Fred Gardaphè sketches a thumbnail self-portrait of his life as he reflects on his experiences in therapy following his marital breakup. He discusses the Italian American family, masculinity, mother-son relations, and growing up in a tough Chicago neighborhood in relationship to his treatment. He recounts his experiences with honesty, openness, and insightfulness, and his tale reads like a Hemmingway short story.

Part III looks at theoretical perspectives and treatment issues for Italian Americans. Like many other white ethnic groups, Italian Americans have had a unique history and a distinctive immigration experience to the United States. Many professionals in the mental health field, however, make the assumption that Italian Americans have values consonant with mainstream Americans. It is essential that mental health professionals have some understanding of Italian American culture, and that they address the issue of culture in the context of treatment.

In the first essay of this part, Kathryn Alessandria and Maria Kopacz discuss the concept of ethnic identity, look at the cultural identity of Italian Americans, and examine the persistence of Italian American cultural values in the postimmigrant population. They conclude the essay by providing an extensive set of practical tools that professionals can incorporate into culturally sensitive counseling services for Italian American clients.

In the next essay, Donna DiCello and Lorraine Mangione examine the topic of grief and loss in the Italian American community. While death is a universal experience for all ethnic groups, the way Italian Americans deal with this issue may not fit with expectations from conventional psychology. DiCello and Mangione pose questions about the Italian American experience of death, provide concepts about Italian Americans and their relationship to death, and offer ideas about metaphors that they regard as central to their view of working with grief and loss. The authors share their own personal stories of how they have dealt with the death of their fathers, outline clinical applications of grief work for both the general population and for Italian Americans, and discuss a case example of an Italian American woman who sought mental health treatment from one of the authors.

Next, Lorraine Mangione and Rachel McBride explore Italian American women's identity development through the lens of poetry. They look at factors that may be important for the formation and evolution of Italian American women's identity, and the issues, conflicts, strengths, values, and experiences that might make up their identity. They comprehensively examine poetry and identity development via object relations and life span development theories, as well as through acculturation. Interspersed throughout the essay are poems by Italian American women. The essay concludes with suggestions for working with Italian American women regarding issues of identity.

In the final essay of this book, Anthony Tasso, Dana Kaspereen-Guidicipietro, and Jennifer Tursi investigate the topic of domestic violence in the Italian American community. They provide an overview of domestic violence, describe Italian and Italian American cultural themes, and offer a detailed examination of how Italian American cultural factors may interact with psychological phenomena that are relevant to domestic violence. They bring the essay to a close by outlining domestic violence treatment implications for Italian Americans, and by proffering their conclusions about current research and theory on domestic violence and its applicability to the Italian American population.

This volume is an essential tool for any mental health practitioner who may be working with Italian American clients. It will also be extremely valuable to clinicians whose practice includes individuals who may share some cultural similarities with Italian Americans. For the researcher, it is a treasure trove of information. The knowledge contained within is indispensible to anyone carrying out research on the Italian American population. The topics that are covered should prove to be fertile ground for further exploration and examination. It is hoped that this book will stimulate further dialogue and study on the subject of Italian American mental health.

DOMINICK CARIELLI

John D. Calandra Italian American Institute

References

Famous Quotes and Authors 2011.
http://famousquotesandauthors.com/authors/william_menninger_quotes.html

PART ONE

Culture and Identity

Cultural Authenticity and Personality Development: The Italian American Example

RICHARD GAMBINO

"Before ye seek to know me, let me know myself."
— Shakespeare, *Venus and Adonis*

I last had the honor of speaking before the Italian American counselors of the City University of New York, together with other clinical psychologists and social work clinicians, in 1988. How to characterize the zeitgeist regarding Italian Americans in the twenty-two years since then? Perhaps with a likely story, a conversation between a person and God:

PERSON: Lord, will there ever be an end to war?
GOD: Yes, but not in your lifetime.
PERSON: Will there ever be an end to famine?
GOD: Yes, but not in your lifetime.
PERSON: My Lord, will there ever be an end to the routine defamation of Italian Americans?
GOD: Yes, but not in my lifetime.

The point of view in this essay starts with this situation and rests on a foundation of three ancient premises. One, that the Socratic maxim, "Know thyself," is wise and is essential to a good life. Two, going further, Boethius was right when he said, "In other creatures ignorance of self is natural; in humankind it is vice." The third premise comes from Marcus Aurelius: "The mind is dyed by the colors of its thoughts."

Going beyond these to more modern insights, a person's sense of self is substantially formed and evolves—to the extent that it evolves—by his or her experience of his or her personal culture vis-à-vis virtual reality views of that culture given to that person by the larger culture. The virtual depictions of his or her culture given by society, and their relationship to his or her authentic reality, may run from very accurate, and positively useful, to highly inaccurate, and personally damaging. In other words, a personality's characteristics, and in turn how the person lives his or her life, are heavily influenced by the larger culture's view of his or her personal culture.

Regarding the Italian American, the prevailing virtual reality affecting his or her sense of self and what he or she can and should do with his or her life represents a kind of Italian American exceptionalism. However, it is an exceptionalism that is more of a curse than a mere distinction. Today, when crude negative stereotypes of other groups, and even when the subtlest and slightest negative stereotypes of them, are perceived, they are vigorously and righteously condemned. Yet, at the same time, Italian Americans are an extremely conspicuous exception. Two slurs of Italian Americans, gross in extremes, which go back to the late nineteenth century, still pervade American culture—and because of the great influence of American culture, they pervade worldwide culture as well. Indeed, they have grown stronger with each generation. For example, the slurs became common on a nationwide and international basis in the events before and after the lynching of eleven Italian Americans in New Orleans on March 14, 1891. I describe this incident in my book *Vendetta* (Gambino 1977).

The first, of course, consists of the constant depictions, descriptions, and suggestions that the historic and present Italian American culture is distinctly and uniquely criminal—the incessant mafia slur. The most recent, highly esteemed, and extremely popular example of this is *The Sopranos* TV show. (Last August, as I was perusing the Amazon website, a pop-up ad appeared featuring what it termed, "Back to school posters." Very prominently displayed was a poster consisting of a photograph of the "Soprano family.") Apologists for the highly celebrated, award-winning show, who cite its well-written scripts and great acting, would not, and do not, justify or excuse slurs against other groups on these grounds. A long-ago parallel is the 1915 silent film, *Birth of a Nation*, depicting crude defamation of African Americans that was very much celebrated and very much justified on the grounds that its director, D.W. Griffith, was a great movie maker. Again, because of the universal influence of American culture, the mafia slur has been for a long time an international standard. For example, I recently watched an entertaining 2009 feature film made in Israel, *A Matter of Size*, in which, in one scene, some Israelis discuss whether "there is mafia in Japan."

The Italian word has been made into a worldwide synonym in countless cultures and languages for any and every kind of organized crime, never mind that any crime that involves more than one criminal is organized. For example, the American media routinely refer to "the Mexican mafia" and "the Russian mafia." Of course, every young person soon learns that the words *mob* and *family* are code words used in referring to criminal groups only when they involve Italian Americans; giving the alleged nicknames of criminals in quotation marks is also reserved for Italian American criminals. These latter are, thus, made to seem to have a uniquely colorful criminality.

This last point brings us to the second slur, now also well over a century old and not only tolerated but celebrated in each generation, the concept of Italian Americans as low-life, laughable, absurd, contemptible, stupid, and mentally, characterologically, and culturally deficient, and/or distorted, fools and buffoons. The present highly popular example of this is found in the TV reality show, *Jersey Shore*. Its characters are depicted as crude, stupid, youngish adults leading pitifully laughable dead-end lives. They are all portrayed as Italian Americans, but according to newspaper reports, some of these people are in reality not Italian American. What's more, *Jersey Shore* is the most watched TV show among people eighteen to forty-nine years old ("Tired of Reality TV" 2010), years that are critical to personality development in individuals. On October 26, 2010, a front-page story in the *Wall Street Journal* ("Ghosts Aren't Nearly as Frightening as These Characters") indicated that the indoctrination of children in the defamation of Italian Americans — compare the "Back to school" Sopranos poster — is keeping pace with the general cultural norm. It began (1):

> What's the scariest part of Halloween this year?
> *Jersey Shore* costumes are topping many retailers' lists as the most popular outfit of the season.
> It's the first Halloween since the notorious MTV reality show, featuring a pack of raucous Italian American twenty-somethings, began airing last December.

In July 2010, the governor of New Jersey appeared on the ABC TV *This Week* program. According to newspaper reports, he objected to *Jersey Shore* — his objection being that the people on the show are not really Jerseyites. He was quoted as saying that the show "takes a bunch of New Yorkers, drops them at the Jersey Shore and tries to make America feel like this is New Jersey." ("NJ Guv Blasts MTV's 'Shore'" 2010). Following this, newspapers in the next few days carried friendly banter between the governors of New Jersey and New York about which state *Jersey Shore* slurs, with both politicians seemingly oblivious to the show's defamation of Italian Americans.

Thus, the larger, now worldwide, culture, says to Italian Americans, with great, authoritative insistence, that its slanderous virtual reality of their culture is more "true" than any contrary sense they may have about their Italian American culture. For example, should one of them assert that his is a family-oriented culture, this brings on snickers and sniggers. Moreover, any objection by a single Italian American or group of them to the nonstop slander and libel is dismissed as psychological denial and defensiveness, or even as proof that Italian Americans are in fact as mentally limited, distorted, or as characterologically warped as the virtual reality depicts them. The effects are to isolate, stigmatize, and marginalize those who speak out, to nullify their objections, and by succeeding in these to deter any others who might speak out. It is much safer to say, as some Italian Americans do, "It doesn't matter. Ignore it;" or, as is the stance of many others — say nothing at all, no matter how irritating the slurs, or on the part especially of young people, how confusing and anxiety-producing the defamation. The resulting feelings are worthlessness, helplessness, and rage.

In 2010, a large university in New York State sponsored an essay contest among Italian American students in high schools who identify in positive ways with their Italian American culture. The students' essays show them to be highly aware, to say the least, of *The Sopranos* and *Jersey Shore* slurs, and very concerned, troubled, or outraged by them.

In short, the defamation of Italian Americans constitutes a system that is extremely pronounced, universal, self-validating, self-reinforcing, and regarded as incontrovertible. In a word, it constitutes a dogma, and an extremely virulent one at that. Yet, every system needs energy to keep going, and systemic anti-Italian American defamation is fueled by the psychological benefits and financial rewards it provides to many people. One, the dogma provides a comforting sense of pseudo-superiority connected to most defamations of groups. People have an excuse, that is always easily available and instantly accessible, to make them feel better about their failures in life, real or perceived, failures in work or careers, personal life, parenting, marriage; in fact, anything and everything. It is the age-old benefit that underlies all group defamations. Racism against African Americans and anti-Semitism are two other common examples, but now both of these are seen as extremely immoral and politically incorrect, unlike anti–Italian American defamation. "No matter how I've failed or messed up," a person's ego says (rarely with full consciousness, but usually semiconsciously or unconsciously), "I'm still better than them." This common psychological dynamic was indentified in its general sense as long ago as 1851, when Herman Melville (1979) in *Moby Dick* had Ishmael say, " – truly to enjoy bodily warmth, some small part of you must be cold, for there is no quality in this world that is not what it is merely by contrast. Nothing exists by itself" (55).

Two, it becomes acceptable to emulate these stereotypes and engage in fantasy syndromes. People can act out what they see on TV shows and everywhere else, including acting out by some Italian Americans themselves, perhaps including some of the people we see in reality TV series like *Jersey Shore*. "I'm tough, macho, sexy, and powerful." Related to this, there's the Walter Mitty fantasy syndrome for many individuals of all backgrounds: "I can live thoughtlessly and just have a good time," just like the idiots on *Jersey Shore*. Even more, I can at least fantasize about being beyond good and evil, beyond all laws; powerful, like the mafia guys on *The Sopranos*. "How I'd like to eliminate anyone I hate or anyone who is in my way like they do; be rich, and have a family life in which I'm important!"

These types of psychological benefits to hundreds of millions of individuals produce a great financial potential – people will buy what builds and reinforces the psychological benefits for them. Hundreds of millions of people, and corporations, and institutions pay for films, TV shows, journalistic stories, books, and the like, capitalizing (literally) on one or both of the two categories of slurs on Italian Americans. In fact, the public can't get enough. After *The Godfather* novel and films we have *The Sopranos*. But is anyone surprised by this? "The Fonz"—the nickname of a very popular and very celebrated laughable, fictional low-life character, "Arthur Fonzarelli," one of a long line of Italian Americans portrayed as buffoons, on the TV show, *Happy Days*, which ran from 1974 to 1984—just opened up greater possibilities for *Jersey Shore*; again, no surprise. (Not to mention the countless others of today's examples in both the mafia and low-life jerks categories.) As demonstrated in generation after generation, writers, producers, directors, actors (each group conspicuously including some Italian Americans), and all whose livings depend on what they do can and do become rich and famous by creating and marketing defamatory mythologies about Italian Americans that are in demand. Moreover, Italian Americans who become rich and famous by exploiting the negative stereotypes are actually honored, instead of criticized, by some Italian American organizations, in a perverse example of celebrity worship or perhaps in some cases they are examples of indulgence of the kind of basking in the Walter Mitty-type fantasies already described. It is necessary to rebuke Italian Americans involved in the defamation of the group, whether they are motivated by hope of material gain, by personal vanity, self-loathing, or cynical weariness. Without them, the strength of the slurs would be much diminished. Imagine an effective coalition of Italian American high achievers and celebrities finally saying in public, "No, this defamation is unacceptable." In fact, the evidence to this day shows that the financial potential in exploiting the myths about Italian Americans is enormous and still growing. (A myth is an account, or in today's jargon, a narrative, of something that may have a grain of truth in it, but, through inventiveness, goes far beyond this grain, sometimes to fantastic extremes. Yes, there have been and are now Italian American gangsters, as there have been and are of every other sizable group; and yes, some Italian Americans are low-lifes, but so are some of every other sizable group.)

Mark Twain was right when he said, "History does not repeat itself, but it does rhyme." These deafening defamations distort the psychological hearing of Italian Americans in their youth and throughout their lives. They can't get the rhymes their lives are to their authentic culture because of the high-decibel, omnipresent noise from the virtual culture in which they live. (For some Italian Americans, the defamatory slurs fill a vacuum that is their lack of educated knowledge of the group's historical and present realities.)

These false and toxic cultural mythologies and the deafness or numbness they produce form an important part of the matrix of influences that bear upon the formation of Italian Americans' personalities from before puberty and the development of these through life to old age. Erik Erikson's (1963) landmark book, *Childhood and Society*, has long been one of the most esteemed works on the subject. In a section of the book entitled "Identity vs. Role Confusion," Erikson says of the age group from twelve to eighteen years of age:

The growing and developing youths, faced with a physiological revolution within them, and with tangible adult tasks ahead of them are now primarily concerned with what they appear to be in the eyes of others as compared with what they feel they are . . . In their search for a new sense of continuity and sameness, adolescents have to refight many of the battles of earlier years, even though to do so they must artificially appoint perfectly well-meaning people to play the roles of adversaries; and they are ever ready to install lasting idols and ideals as guardians of a final identity. (261)

The degree to which the pervasive slurs against Italian Americans affect any given individual among them varies, of course. It is hard to measure what any given individual's personality would have been, and how well it would have served him or her, had these influences not been present. (It's a case of an historical hypothetical; e.g., like that of trying to know how American history would have been different if Abraham Lincoln had not been assassinated.) However, in the field of psychology there is a consensus regarding problems of personality formation and development. Part of the consensus is that confusion has deleterious effects on personality formation and development. The kind of confusion and distraction inflicted on Italian Americans from childhood into adulthood by the virtual culture they are told is their true reality versus their actually experienced personal cultural reality, the confusion born of experiencing two conflicting realties at once. Such confusion produces in Italian Americans behaviors associated with anxiety, doubt, shame, withdrawal, acting out, anger and rage, defiance, resignation, and depression—all the classic symptoms, if you will, of basic personality or identity confusion. Again, which of these, or which mixtures of these, and the degrees of their virulence, differs from individual to individual, but the results are also classic in clinical psychology: All of them result in an individual being self-distorting, self-limiting, and self-defeating.

So we have had historically, and have today, Italian Americans who short-change themselves, being less than they could be in the first stages of life. Later, we see stagnation of self or personality, dullness, or depression, or a sense of resignation by middle age or before, and problems that are characteristic of what personality confusion creates in relationships throughout life—problems with parents, spouses, colleagues, and children—and, in fact, with life in general.

The therapy for the syndromes just described must involve the constituents essential to all therapy. First, there must be an accurate assessment and understanding of the problem by the individual—perhaps helped to this in counseling or formal therapy. Next, the individual must come to know himself or herself, particularly to know and evaluate all the influences that make up the matrix of those that have shaped his or her personality. The goal is gradual self-knowledge and, through it, the goal of all therapeutic psychology—that of the alleviation of a person's suffering from his or her self-limiting psychological problems through gradual insight. Good counseling in school or college contexts can start and guide a person on the path to this self-knowledge. Of course, reading about, and the study of, the authentic history and culture of Italian Americans is of vital importance here.

It might be hard for some to grasp or to accept that the cultural context, and hence the psychological context, of a large group of people can be as absurd as is that created by the now routine and pervasive defamation of Italian Americans, but it should be less so for Italian Americans themselves. For most, by far, are descendants of the history and culture of southern Italy. The role of people in northern Italy in initiating the defamation of Italian Americans—the great majority of whom are of southern Italian origin—is described in my books, *Blood of My Blood* (Gambino 1974) and *Vendetta* (Gambino 1977). A current version of that bigotry is seen in Italy's political party, The Northern League, whose former leader, Umberto Bossi, said that people in northern Italy "descend from northern Celtic tribes . . . a hard working people," in contrast to the lazy, irresponsible Italians to the south who "steal jobs" from the north ("An Italian Firebrand" 2010).

One of the characteristic wisdoms of that historical culture was summed up by the great Sicilian playwright, Luigi Pirandello (1922), in his famous play, *Six Characters in Search of an Author*, a play about the formation of personality; a play whose first performance in cosmopolitan Rome in 1921 caused a near riot in the theater in which it was performed, with audience members yelling, among other, less printable things, "Madness!" As one of the play's characters puts it, ". . . life is full of infinite absurdities, which strangely enough, do not even need to be plausible, since they are true" (9). This as well as the relationship to the overlying moral imperative that lies in the three ancient premises from Socrates, Boethius, and Marcus Aurelius stated at the beginning of this paper — for it is also said, by the character The Father, in Pirandello's play:

> Every true man, sir, who is a little above the level of the beasts and plants does not live for the sake of living, without knowing how to live; but he lives so as to give a meaning and value to his own life. For me this is everything. (64)

References

Erikson, Erik H. 1963. *Childhood and Society*, 2nd ed., New York: W.W. Norton.

Gambino, Richard. 1974. *Blood of My Blood*. New York. Doubleday. Now published by Guernica Editions: New York and Toronto.

_____. 1977. *Vendetta*. New York: Doubleday. Now published by Guernica Editions: New York and Toronto.

Maymon, Sharon, and Erez Tadmor. 2009. *A Matter of Size*. Israel.

Melville, Herman. 1979. *Moby Dick*. Berkeley: University of California Press. (original work published in 1851).

Pirandello, Luigi. 2009. (E. Storer, Trans.). *Six Characters in Search of an Author*. Digireads.com.

"An Italian Firebrand Gains Votes, Power in Crisis." 2010. *The Wall Street Journal*. December 13.

"Ghosts Aren't Nearly as Frightening as These Characters." 2010. *The Wall Street Journal*. October 26.

"NJ Guv Blasts MTV's 'Shore.'" 2010. *Newsday*. July 26.

"Tired of Reality TV, But Still Tuning In." 2010. *The New York Times Online*. Accessed September 13.

Being White, Feeling Black, Acting Out: Identity Development Among Italian American Youth

DONNA M. CHIRICO

INTRODUCTION AND THEORETICAL FRAMEWORK

Let me begin by asking two questions:

> 1. How do you identify with respect to ethnicity? Do you say American? Or, do you say Italian American, German Irish American, Italian German (fill-in-the-blank) American?
> 2. Do you think of yourself as white or black?

In the last decade, the question that has fueled my research program asks: Why haven't Americans of Italian descent achieved the educational attainment levels of other European ethnic groups? This research program focuses upon assessing what I call exoteric or secular imagination and the esoteric or transcendent imagination. The underlying hypothesis is that the thinking outside the box dimension, the esoteric imagination, is what motivates the individual to attain higher or more complex levels of development. The box to get out of in this case is ethnicity. This work focuses on looking at the ability to transcend obstacles that ultimately permit individuals to achieve enriched levels of personal or transcendent development that are essential for mental health and wellness. Often, the barriers are created by ethnic traditions that set boundaries within which the person must remain to be accepted by those of shared ethnicity. As this work has progressed, certain parallels between Italian Americans and other lower-achieving ethnic groups have become apparent. There are strikingly similar patterns between Italian Americans and African Americans, where cultural practices and religious participation can become the stumbling blocks to transcendence. This essay examines the influence of culture and social structures, including the structures imposed by participating in a religion and the resulting sense of identity, or better put confused identity, that emerges leading to behaviors that struggle against mainstream culture and societal norms confining the individual to only ethnically acceptable patterns of identity.

Since I first embarked on the study of imagination in the late 1990s, its significance within the study of mainstream psychology is still marginal. The importance of transcendent imagination as related to religious inclination is largely ignored as a factor central to overall psychological development and mental health. Certainly, there is no linkage to the place of religiosity in the emergence of identity. If there is doubt about this point, look at any standard college textbook on human development or personality theory to discover the palpable absence of reference to any spiritual dimension, despite the backdrop of an American culture where religious participation and professed God beliefs are high.

The presumed universal stage models of cognition and morality do not account directly for the place of imagination and religiosity in the unfolding of identity development; consequently, the religious/spiritual models of psychological maturation lack a full consideration of how a life-long pursuit of imaginative faith influences overall psychological growth. James Fowler (1995) offers a far-reaching explanation about the place of faith in the individual's quest for meaning, but the model has not displaced other developmental theories as the central ideology for individual development. All of the stage models have been seriously challenged in the last decade in favor of social constructivist approaches and those that come out of cognitive science, where psychological development is seen simply as brain development. The influence of ethnicity has emerged as a factor, but the religious dimensions of ethnic traditions are often ignored.

The contention of this research assumes that imagination manifests itself through two complimentary aspects: (1) An exoteric or secular dimension of imagination that operates in conjunction with (2) an esoteric or transcendent dimension of imagination. Both are essential to the creation of inner life. The secular dimension emerges from interaction with culture and social structures; but it is the latter spiritual imagination that serves as the catalyst in transcending the everyday and is central to achieving ultimate goals. It is the way we surmount the limitations of cultural and social structures. Ultimately, it is the fully developed transcendent imagination that brings about a secure sense of personal identity that permits the person to get outside of the box.

One observable endeavor in line with this thinking that requires persistence in the face of adverse circumstances is the attainment of a college
degree. The hypothesis then becomes: If an individual possesses a heightened capacity for imagination, esoteric or otherwise, this confidence of
personal identity will enable that person to succeed in college despite
shortcomings in the traditional predictive variables such as family background, high school GPA, SAT scores, and intelligence measures. This
applies to individuals from various ethnic groups, especially immigrants
and the children of immigrants (and their grandchildren), including African Americans, Latinos, and certain European immigrants; namely, Italian Americans and Irish Americans who, despite apparent gains in other
success dimensions, still trail others, who claim alternate European ancestries, in educational attainment.

It should come as no surprise that rates of success for all immigrants
with respect to college graduation have increased. It is the "rising tide
raises all ships effect." The numbers overall have improved, but when a
comparative analysis is done assessing the achievements of specific ethnic
groups and the data are pulled apart, a different story emerges. Blacks
have much lower rates of success, as do Hispanics, when compared to
other ethnic groups. If one looks at Italian Americans versus similar
groups who cite European ancestry, then the picture is also less rosy.

TABLE 1. *Selected Educational Attainment of Americans by Ancestry: Bachelor's Degree or Higher*

	FEMALES AGE 25+	MALES AGE 25+
All Americans	26.0%	28.5%
Austrian	42.4%	50.4%
British	51.1%	56.3%
Danish	35.3%	40.4%
European	**52.7%**	**54.2%**
German	30.3%	33.0%
Irish	29.4%	33.1%
Italian	**30.3%**	**33.8%**
Scandinavian	44.2%	47.1%
Scotch-Irish	36.2%	41.5%

Source: United States Census Bureau, *American Community Survey, FactFinder 2005.*

The rate of educational attainment for Italian Americans is higher
than for the American population at large, but this data category includes
all Americans—blacks, Hispanics, recent immigrants, and even undocu-

mented immigrants. When compared to others with similar ethnic histories, that is, other immigrants whose roots lie in the waves of immigration of the late nineteenth and early twentieth centuries, it is evident that Italian Americans have not made the strides of other European immigrants (see Table 1). It is interesting to note that this is also true for Irish Americans who, although not hampered by speaking a different language, share the bonds of the American Roman Catholic Church. Among European immigrants, the success rates for women are lower than for men.

In the case of Irish and Italian Americans, again especially among women, the nature of the Catholic Church in the United States vis-à-vis these groups needs to be factored into the equation. Although the sociology of Irish and Italian American educational failure is more complicated, it is not unfair to state that the Catholic Church has played a central role in this situation. In many ways, the rigid orthodoxy of American Catholic bureaucracy has thwarted the full expression of esoteric imagination among immigrant Americans, who, in the past, used the bureaucracy of the church as the primary outlet of socialization. In an institution still dominated by an Irish American hierarchy, a group that has even lower levels of educational achievement than Italian Americans, others are made to stay in their place. The Archdiocese of New York website, for example, currently lists six out of ten bishops of Irish heritage in a city that has an Irish population of about five percent. (According to the American Community Survey 2005, New York City has a current population where 8.2 percent claim Italian ancestry and 5.2 percent claim Irish ancestry.) German Americans have low rates, too, and one can surmise similarities between the orthodoxy of Catholicism and the Evangelical Lutheran Church in America. Therefore, breaking away from what is assigned and attaining success in the sphere of education may require something exceptional at work regarding this capacity. I am suggesting that this lies in the formation of an independent personal identity.

IDENTITY AND TRANSCENDENT IMAGINATION
AS A FUNCTION OF ETHNICITY

David Bohm tells us that "from time to time, however, challenges arise that require a creative and original response, going beyond the whole field of what can be handled by assimilation within known general framework" (Bohm 1984, 10). Imagination in this way becomes a way of knowing, an epistemological process. As an illustration of how these processes work, Bohm differentiates between "imaginative insights" and "rational insights." Both involve a creative energy and new perception, but the former is a way of describing literary insights as is true in poetry, and the latter refers to the rational insights engendered in science. Bohm's model is, in part, building upon the poet Samuel Taylor Coleridge's idea of fancy versus imagination (Coleridge 2010). This is an acknowledgment that imagination has dimensions within it corresponding to the prosaic and the transcendent. There is a light-hearted component that acts in or near the surface of consciousness and a formative constituent that does its work deeper into the psyche.

Coleridge created his scheme to differentiate the poet of talent from the poet of genius. Fancy is strictly an associative process. The raw materials of cognition — sensation, perception, memory, recognition, information processing, and the like — are woven and rewoven to create interesting outcomes, but each outcome is a mirror of experience. Imagination is a creative process. The raw materials of experience are broken down, re-created and given new structure. The result is unique, so that the "artistic imagination creates a new world; one like the everyday world of perception, but reorganized and raised to a higher level of universality" (Brett 1969, 42). Unity is created rather than duality in all things. What is being suggested is that imagination is not merely an additional component of psychological development but the original ingredient without which identity would not develop.

It is the strength of the transcendent imagination that fosters authentic development with a unity of psychological functions. Without this, the individual remains trapped in the conventional roles ethnicity assigns. Family and religious participation shape these. If it is true, as previous studies seem to confirm, that social roles are organized around the family and that these roles are reinforced by the bureaucratic structure of the churches in America, and, further, that it is the Catholic Church with which the majority of Italian Americans are affiliated, then it follows that individuals who exhibit a transcendent imagination should be able to go outside the traditional roles of ethnicity, assigned by family and church, more easily.

Understanding this situation first requires an awareness of the history of failure in longer-term immigrants in the African American, Latino, and Italian American communities. Each group has had its own cultural and social barriers to surmount. In black communities it has been the disruption of family structure, a legacy of slavery, and racism; in Hispanic communities English as a second language is a factor; and in the Italian American community there has been an antipathy toward education first expressed by the initial Italian immigrant community. All three groups experience aspects of each other's problems: Family, language, and misgivings about the value of education. In reference to this last problem, the educator Leonard Covello once stated: "The most overt conflict between the American school and the Italian parental home seems to derive from the economic values of Italian family life . . . Thus the old world tradition which demands of the child a share in the economic upkeep of the family, regardless of the child's age and capacity, was invoked in America" (1967, 403–404). This disposition persists as Italian Americans have achieved economic success in the new world, yet still lag with regard to educational attainment. The fields of educational success are often vocational professions in character such as medicine and the law, which are considered respectable academic pursuits because there is a perceived relationship with economic success.

A point that Covello (1967) alludes to is the wariness Italian immigrants in the early twentieth century had toward both the bureaucratic structures of society and the figures of authority controlling those structures. In *Where You Stand Depends on Where Your Grandparents Sat*, Eric Uslaner (2008) gives us a way of understanding this sense of caution by explaining the significance of "generalized trust." Generalized trust is a stable value that emerges through the developmental process and is gained through interaction with one's parents. Those familiar with Erik Erikson's (1968) model of psychosocial development know that Trust versus Mistrust is the first stage of that model, whose successful completion relies on a positive nurturing experience between parent/primary caregiver and the infant. Uslaner's (2008) work tells us that Italians, Latinos, and blacks have lower levels of generalized trust than do people of Nordic, German, or British origins. While the individual may come to trust the primary caregiver and even the immediate community of caregivers, ethnic heritage has a strong influence on one's broader sense of trust. Going to, and persisting to graduate from, college entails much generalized trust in the system, in your professors, in your peers, and in the acceptance of the idea that having a college degree is better than not having one for success in life.

While it is generally accepted that the individual must develop a sense of personal identity as a prolegomenon to the trajectory of overall individual development [see Erikson and Erikson (1998), Marcia (1980), and Waterman (1982)], the specifics of what leads to this development in the context of race and ethnicity is still not clear when looking at specific ethnic subgroups. Erikson established identity as the psychosocial accomplishment of adolescence, and, although Tajfel, Henri, and Turner (1979) argued that identity development as filtered through a social group identity perspective could have negative effects if that group is devalued in the majority culture, later research does not support this assertion. In general, the effort to link the level of negative societal regard toward any specific ethnic group with aspects of the individual's internalized self-evaluation for traits such as self-esteem are not supported (Twenge and Crocker 2002). A difficulty in counseling and educational settings, for example, is the widely held, yet false, belief that encountering racial or cultural insensitivity leads to a lowered sense of self-esteem. There are various levels of difficulty with this premise. An exploration of the current research programs and the problems within research designs indicates that much of the work in this area is cross sectional rather than longitudinal, and late adolescence is the focus, rather than early to middle adolescence (French et al. 2006). Indeed, a special issue of the *Journal of Counseling Psychology* was published in 2007 citing "the need for a scholarly dialogue among leading researchers to help clarify . . . issues and provide guidance to a new generation of multicultural researchers" (Ponterotto and Mallinckrodt 2007, 219). There is additionally the failure to parse ethnicity and make distinctions; the category "white" is a broad one that encompasses divergent experiences. The variables have proven to be much more complex than first imagined. In my own work, I have cited the negative effects of societal structures as they interact with ethnic variables, specifically the impact of the American Roman Catholic Church in the lives of Italian Americans (Chirico 2001), but I have not looked at whether there are benefits to identity development of having a specific internalized Italian American identity. The matter becomes more convoluted when the literature is thoroughly examined because different ethnic/racial groups seem to respond differently to the perceived majority culture. Whether having defining racial and ethnic identities is a benefit to the process of actualization is central in identity research, as the negative connotations regarding maintaining one's ethnic mores has dissipated. The concept that assimilation precludes maintaining ethnic ties is out of date.

The two major competing theories that attempt to explain how ethnicity and identity interact are the social identity theory and the multicultural theory. The social identity theory argues that as the individual comes to identify more strongly with his/her own group, the less favorably the individual comes to view other groups (Tajfel and Turner 1979). In social psychology, this phenomenon has been studied under the rubrics of us/them or the in-group/out-group experience. These studies generally indicate that being among the in-group creates an unfavorable attitude or prejudice toward anyone outside the group. Researchers have used myriad in-group/out-group contrivances, ranging from serious issues such as white versus black racial divisions to those that may at first seem trivial (Devine 1989; Dudley and Mulvey 2009).

The difficulty is when the aversion becomes so strong that it prevents the individual from exploring the mainstream culture, thus limiting personal development and achievement. This becomes a way to explain why a young person brought up with condemnation of the out-group limits interacting with it and taking advantage of what the out-group culture has to offer. It is not uncommon, for example, to meet individuals living in ethnic neighborhoods that would never dream of living anywhere else, or why these ethnic enclaves are re-created when retirement communities elsewhere are constructed. One sees in the latter a similar pattern to ones found in initial immigration patterns to the United States. Just as Italian immigrants of the early twentieth century found their way to a Little Italy in New York City or San Francisco, second- and third-generation Italian Americans found their way to like-minded communities in Naples or Venice, Florida. In certain African American subcultures there is often contempt for blacks seeking an entrée to white society. This is not just the "Uncle Tom" behavior derided in the past and extends to matters of staying in school and career choice.

In contrast, the multicultural theory argues that having strong in-group identification and, by implication, a secure sense of ethnic identity allows the individual to display greater tolerance for the out-group (Berry 1984; Helms 1984). There is no need to berate or avoid the out-group; it is seen as merely different, not objectionable. In this model, having a strong Italian American identity allows a person to explore alternative ways to assimilate or achieve from those particular to the in-group because these would not be seen as repellant or being at odds with Italian American culture per se. One can then accept being Italian American as part of a personal identity that includes other dimensions, as opposed to claiming to be solely Italian American on the basis of what the in-group deems acceptable. This individual is able to live outside the old neighborhood and not feel that doing so threatens personal identity; one can be Italian American and be part of mainstream society simultaneously. This perspective validates Erikson, who argues that this confidence of personal identity first achieved during adolescence through early young adulthood is necessary to furthering identity development through adulthood. In Erikson's system, the positive resolution of each stage of development is marked by the acquisition of a particular ego virtue or ego strength that is necessary for the individual to move into the subsequent stage. The ego strength that culminates the identity formation stage of adolescence is fidelity and is defined as "the ability to sustain loyalties freely pledged in spite of the inevitable contradictions of the value systems" (Erikson 1968, 125). Fidelity gives individuals the wherewithal to become or remain friends with those whose values and beliefs differ from their own. Given the security of personal beliefs in these individuals, there is no perceived threat from those ideas that are in conflict, so moving freely beyond the in-group becomes possible. Parental fear about teenagers associating with friends who may be bad influences is common. Given what is known about role experimentation during adolescence, the fear is not unjustified given that the adolescent has yet to complete the process of identity formation through the requisite identity crisis. The same fear can just as readily create a wariness of the out-group as described in social identity theory, even when the out-group may lead to positive influences.

The Amish and Hasidic communities illustrate the strategy that separation will preserve community ideals and attitudes. In American society at large, it is exceedingly difficult to keep young people away from cultural influences that caregivers may deem inappropriate or detrimental. When the adolescent is not able to work through the identity crisis, one unwanted outcome is what Marcia describes as identity foreclosure. In this case, adolescents fail to work through the identity crisis and instead assume the values and beliefs of others in their sphere of influence (Marcia 1966). Rather than forging their own path, these young people follow the direction set by others. When this happens, further development is stifled and the consequences for later developmental crises are dire. In the present discussion, there is a further pulling back from outside influences that might upend a shaky sense of self, leading to the nonthreatening choice of remaining within the in-group.

Jean Phinney (1996), using Erikson and Marcia as her foundation, developed a stage model for ethnic identity development combining the ideas of exploration and commitment. "Exploration represents the extent to which adolescents seek out the content (language, cultural practices, beliefs) of their ethnic heritage as well as the significance of that ethnic information for their personal identity. Commitment embodies how strongly an adolescent embraces and values ethnicity as a part of personal identity" (Phinney 1996, 148). The path of ethnic identity follows the one theorized by Erikson for ego identity that includes a search that can ultimately lead to identity achievement, which in this model means ethnic identity achievement. While there is some support for a developmental stage model of ethnic identity, it has mostly been used to study the "major" minorities. So, again, the all-embracing category is white, rather than using individual European subgroups.

The debate between social identity theory and multicultural theory continues because neither succeeds as a universal model and because much depends on which ethnic/racial groups are being evaluated. Breaking down the groups as white versus those that are nonwhite does not permit for a careful analysis because the ethnic differences within these categories are enormous. Considering yourself nonwhite engenders different attitudes than when you see yourself as white. Therein lies the conundrum for Italian Americans as they are being discussed and evaluated in the social sciences: Are we to be seen as white or nonwhite? As stated above, little research has been done to explore the subgroups for the category white as it applies to European ancestry. It is typical in research that all are considered as one. Yet, anyone living in a multiethnic environment understands that Italian Americans are different from Greek Americans, who are different from Irish Americans, and so on. Lumping all blacks together makes little sense, too. Yet, this is done, although to a lesser extent and with a broader literature against presenting a single classification. As K. Anthony Appiah has written: "If we follow the badge of color from 'African' to 'Negro' to 'Colored Race' to 'Black' to 'Afro-American' to 'African-American' (and this ignores such fascinating detours as the route by way of 'Afro-Saxon'), we are thus tracing the history of not only a signifier, a label, but also of the history of its effects" (1996, 68). The effects of color are widely examined, but the effects specific to ethnic identity in blacks or whites is rarely the focus. A distinction is made between the two, and it is acknowledged that both are important in the developing adolescent. Racial identity is a socially constructed phenomenon "defined largely by physical differences" whereas ethnic identity is determined through "self-identified affiliation" (Wakefield and Hudley 2007, 148). The former is predetermined for you largely based on how you look, while the latter is a choice of your making. While there is certainly an interaction between race and ethnicity, race is more evidently predetermined because if you are black or white, others will make immediate judgments on seeing the color of your skin. Although attitudes toward ethnic groups are also preconceptions, ethnicity is not readily apparent, especially if you look white; therefore, self-identification is required. Since ethnic identity derives from familial rather than societal influences, a person of mixed ethnicity, say Irish and Italian, will literally choose whether he/she will identity as Irish, Italian, or both. The prejudices encountered depend on your stated identification.

Given what is known about how a person comes to develop a personal identity, it follows that where the expression of ethnicity is diminished within the family, young people will end up using other means such as the families of friends or media sources, like films, television shows, or music videos, for cues to establish ethnic identity. This is one reason why Michael Corleone and Tony Soprano become role models. (Michael Corleone was the heir to the Corleone crime family mantle in Francis Ford Coppola's *Godfather* trilogy and Tony Soprano is the lead character in David Chase's television series about an Italian American mobster from New Jersey.) It is equally clear that the models need not be of the same ethnicity as the young person, which accounts for the various wannabe types. When figures from popular culture become the models, racial boundaries are crossed, too, thus, accounting for white kids emulating rappers and black kids trying on the wiseguy role.

THE VALUE OF AN ITALIAN AMERICAN IDENTITY

There is still a missing element in this analysis and that is the explanation for why a person comes to devalue his or her ethnic group of origin. One response to establishing an ethnic identity is through insulating oneself from the out-group; a second alternative is developing a security in ethnic identity that leaves one free to mingle with the out-group. Neither approach addresses the question: Why do some people choose to disassociate themselves from being considered Italian American or try to pass as white instead of black? The advantages of being white manifest themselves in prejudices within the black community. This is not unjustified, as "blacks with lighter skin have historically had better educational, labor market and marital outcomes than blacks with darker skin" (Gullickson 2005, 157). Generally, when a person manifests self-hatred for aspects of personal identity, this is seen as the result of oppression from the outside. Hence, the two groups for which there is a literature about externally motivated self-hatred are blacks and Jews [Wester et al. (2006) provide an example among blacks, and Rosenwasser (2002) provides an example among Jews]. In coming to understand how ethnic identity contributes to the development of personal identity, one must evaluate the reasons for distancing oneself from ethnicity in a context where there is no history of systematic oppression from the external sphere. Here, instead, the ingroup is the negative, oppressive force. A possible explanation for self-hatred in the Italian American community is the deeper held belief that being Italian American is akin to being nonwhite, and, hence, a greater barrier to assimilation is presented. Certainly, Sicilian immigrants were regularly treated as nonwhite when they first arrived in the United States and experienced the sting of racism as a consequence. Depictions of Sicilian and other Italian immigrants in the media in the early part of the last century show us the negative way they were held by the majority culture. It is not difficult to see the continuance of this negative stereotyping in the imagery of Italian Americans in contemporary America, where images of mobsters far outnumber images of Italian American scholars in their academic robes.

The Italian American community at large has not resolved the controversy of seeing itself as white or nonwhite, but this is true for other issues that have come to diminish a sense of group cohesion where self-identification is missing. The conflict surrounding the way the word *Italian American* should be written demonstrates the basic disagreements that need to be resolved. Anthony Julian Tamburri (1991) has written extensively about the use of the hyphen and suggests using a slash instead (Italian/American), thereby "closing the ideological gap" created when the hyphen physically separates the Italian from the American. The tensions that arise surrounding ethnic identity in the aggregate reflect upon development of the individual. This trait is shared, too, with African Americans. Neither has a clearly expressed unified group identity.

In support of Erikson, it has been found that exploring racial and ethnic identity roles is part of the normative process of identity formation. It is often disconcerting for parents when emerging teenagers go through this needed role-playing stage, but it is vital that this process occurs or the consequence is one of several negative identity outcomes. It is therefore necessary to see the importance of Fred Gardaphé's (2006) *From Wiseguys to Wise Men* in this regard, so that we understand that in order eventually to be a wise man, one must first experiment with being a wiseguy. Instead of using what is known about identity experimentation to foster development, there is a tendency to concede to the pressures of cultural relativism and accept the experimentation as the final product. The concern should not be the process, but who the young person will emulate during the process. As numerous studies have concluded, in order for parental values to be internalized, "first, children must perceive the values their parents endorse" (Knafo and Schwartz 2004, 440). There are no guarantees that parental values will be preferred, but if there are no clearly defined, positive racial or ethnic roles in the teenager's environment, that teenager must look to other sources, and the media is happy to provide them.

There are now several ongoing longitudinal studies exploring multiple outcomes for immigrant groups where the importance for held values can be seen as leading to positive or negative outcomes. It is understood that the word *immigrant* does not apply to all African Americans living in the United States, or, perhaps, not even for third- or fourth-generation descendants of immigrants, but for want of a better designation it is being used here as a generic term for outsider. It must be remembered too that since the Civil War era there have been waves of black immigrants who did not come as slaves. A particular combination of factors can be used to predict who is likely to achieve versus who is likely to fail across valued indicators of success among immigrants, but I shall focus only on educational success.

The Children of Immigrants Longitudinal Study (CILS) is the most significant longitudinal study done exploring paths of immigrant success (Portes and Rimbaud 2006). In the CILS, it was found that the lowest rates of educational attainment were found among Mexican and Cambodian/Laotian immigrants, while the highest were among Chinese. This is measured by average years of education completed, with 13.3 years for the former and 15.4 for the latter. While the current immigrant study does not focus on European immigrants or African Americans, the variables that are found to create a significant impact in immigrant success, including educational attainment, are factors that have had a great impact on African Americans and, based on the similarities previously discussed, by extension, Italian Americans. These include:

1. LANGUAGE PREFERENCE AND PROFICIENCY: Bilingualism has shown to be an advantage, but there must be proficiency in each language. Whether one speaks with an accent or not, speaking English is a factor—still. One must consider the urban patois used by black and Italian Americans as an accent. This may not be a hindrance in the music or television industries, but it certainly becomes an impediment in settings of higher education.

2. FAMILY INCOME: Family income is a major factor in overall educational attainment, but this is because money provides the means for caregivers to send their children to private schools. There is a substantial difference in the performance of those who go to private schools as compared to public schools through the high school years (Braun, Jenkins, and Grigg 2006). Hence, many low-income families will strive to provide a private school education, even if this means making other sacrifices to find the money for increasingly rising tuitions. This helps to explain why the proportion of immigrant children at New York City's selective high schools is so high. Just go to any of these schools the day the admissions tests are given and see who is there. The reliance of Italian Americans and blacks on parochial schools, as opposed to secular private schools, needs to be considered as a function of this process. These institutions provide an educational advantage, yet allow participants to stay within the monastery walls, so to speak; one may come to trust those in your immediate surroundings who are familiar to you, while limiting the general trust outside these boundaries.

3. MARRIAGE AND PARENTHOOD: One of clearest links to educational attainment is the age at which a person marries and then has children. The second-generation immigrant groups with the lowest rates of educational attainment are those who have children at a young age. The CILS data tell us that at average age twenty-four, none of the Chinese subjects had children (although some were married or partnered), but twenty-five percent of

Cambodians/Laotians had children and forty-one percent of se-cond-generation Mexicans had children. Again, the influence of Catholicism with its sanctified view toward marriage becomes a factor for Mexicans and Italian Americans, where there is pressure for early marriage and divorce is discouraged.

4. ARRESTS AND INCARCERATION: Ending up in jail is a more complex factor to analyze. Currently, the most alarming rates are among immigrants from Mexico and the West Indies. The rates are substantially higher among men. The continuing racial dis-proportionality of incarceration is supported by a vast literature. (All data from the Children of Immigrants Longitudinal Study are available online at http://cmd.princeton.edu/cils%20iii.shtml.)

In returning to the question of whether Italian Americans are seen as white or nonwhite, it should be apparent that identifying with either group serves no purpose without exploring the salience of identification to individual development. In every group, the individual members are at different planes of experience, but there must be acknowledgement that one does not simply stop changing and growing at any level. I would argue that the remarkable interest in ethnic group nostalgia stems from the insecurities associated with the fear of moving beyond the present in-group expectations and desire to change, perhaps actualize. The white versus nonwhite question inevitably frames the approach to formulating hypotheses and engaging in the needed research.

This question needs to be addressed, taking into account the variables of race, ethnicity, and religion simultaneously. This will depend upon whether or not Italian American researchers can come to terms with the marginalized place of Italian Americans as a subject pool. As I have pre-viously stated elsewhere (Chirico 2001), this requires overcoming three faulty ideas. The first is that Italian Americans are a subgroup not worth individualized study because Italians are white and share the same social constructions of identity as all other white groups. A second is the worry that the aspects studied only serve to perpetuate stereotypes about Italian Americans, so looking at Italian American kids who adopt the wiseguy persona may further encourage group stereotypes. A third has to do with the self-hatred within ethnic communities, so that studying Italian Amer-icans means admitting that we are not part of the majority culture – that we are different. Yet, coming to understand the development of ethnic identity in Italian Americans is critical because when all is said, "one of the clearest findings from research on the development of ethnic and racial identity confirms that ethnic identity has a positive relationship with self-esteem for adolescents from various racial and ethnic backgrounds" (Wakefield and Hudley 2007, 150).

The hyphens of ethnicity are essential to development. A positive identity comes to be formed through understanding the place of racial and ethnic identity within that structure. In doing so, it is also essential in understanding that race and ethnicity are bound up together in ways not easily discerned. This being the case, the American Anthropological Association proposed that race be excised as a category in its report describing how data collection should be carried out for the 2010 United States Census. Although not adopted, the Association recommended, "the elimination of the term 'race' . . . during the planning for the 2010 Census. During the past fifty years, 'race' has been scientifically proven to not be a real, natural phenomenon. More specific, social categories such as 'ethnicity' or 'ethnic group' are more salient for scientific purposes and have fewer of the negative, racist connotations for which the concept of race was developed" (1997, para. 40). This makes it critical to come to terms with how ethnicity is discussed, measured, and studied as psychologists and others try to formulate theories about furthering our understanding of personal identity and the status of ethnic identity. This is necessary in order to determine how ethnic identity as a reflection of race contributes to the positive development of personal identity. The hyphens of ethnicity and race are part of the mix in our society and, therefore, must be considered as factors salient in fostering psychological development, mental health, and general well-being. It seems we are finally recognizing that personal identity is in part defined by ethnicity as it comes to us through our in-group and through the judgment of the out-group, making it one more defining element that must be considered. What is needed among researchers is the ability to imaginatively break free from previously established categories and transcend the dynamics of race and ethnicity to find a way to help individuals move toward a fully realized sense of self that brings with it a confidence of belonging and a harmony of psychological functioning. Continued pursuit looking at the difference between the exoteric and esoteric imagination is one way to achieve this goal.

References

American Anthropological Association. 1997. "Race and Ethnic Standards for Federal Statistics and Administrative Reporting." Response to OMB directive. Available at: http://www.aaanet.org/gvt/ombdraft.htm.

Appiah, K. Anthony. 1996. "Reconstructing Racial Identities." *Research in African Literatures.* 27(3):68–72.

Berry, John W. 1984. "Cultural Relations in Plural Societies: Alternatives to Segregation and Their Sociopsychological Implications." In *Groups in Contact: The Psychology of Desegregation,* edited by Norman Miller and Marilyn Brewer, 111–129. Orlando, FL: Academic Press.

Bohm, David. 1984. "Insight, Knowledge, Science, and Human Values," in *Toward the Recovery of Wholeness,* edited by Douglas Sloan, 8–30. New York: Teachers College Press.

Braun, Henry, Frank Jenkins, and Wendy Grigg. 2006. U.S. Department of Education, National Center for Education Statistics, Institute of Education Sciences. *Comparing Private Schools and Public Schools Using Hierarchical LinearModeling (NCES 2006-461).* Washington, DC: U.S. Government Printing Office.

Brett, R. L. 1969. *Fancy and Imagination.* London: Methuen.

Chirico, Donna. 2001. "Exoteric and Esoteric Imagination in Psychological Development." *Social Compass* 48(4):525–539.

Coleridge, Samuel Taylor. 2010. *Biographia Literaria.* Lenox, Massachusetts: Hard Press Publishing.

Covello, Leonard. 1967. *The Social Background of the Italo-American School Child.* Leiden, Netherlands: E.J. Brill.

Devine, Patricia G. 1989. "Stereotypes and Prejudice: Their Automatic and Controlled Components." *Journal of Personality and Social Psychology* 56(1):5–18.

Dudley, Michael G., and Daniel Mulvey. 2009. "Differentiating Among Outgroups: Predictors of Congruent and Discordant Prejudice." *North American Journal of Psychology* 11(1):143–156.

Erikson, Erik. H. 1968. *Identity, Youth, and Crisis.* New York: Norton.

_____, and Joan M. Erikson. 1998. *The Life Cycle Completed.* New York: W.W. Norton.

Fowler, James. 1995. *Stages of Faith: The Psychology of Human Development and the Quest for Meaning.* San Francisco, CA: HarperOne.

French, Sabine E., Edward Seidman, LaRue Allen, and J. Lawrence Aber. 2006. "The Development of Ethnic Identity During Adolescence." *Developmental Psychology* 42(1):1–10.

Gardaphé, Fred. 2006. *From Wiseguys to Wise Men: The Gangster and Italian American Masculinities.* New York: Taylor and Francis.

Gullickson, Aaron. 2005. "The Significance of Color Declines: A Re-Analysis of Skin Tone Differentials in Post-Civil Rights America." *Social Forces* 84(1):157–180.

Helms, Janet E. 1984. "Towards a Theoretical Explanation of the Effects of Race on Counseling: A Black and White Model." *The Counseling Psychologist* 12(3-4):153–165.

Knafo, Ariel, and Shalom H. Schwartz. 2004. "Identity Formation and Parent-Child Value Congruence in Adolescence." *British Journal of Developmental Psychology* 22(3):439–458.

Marcia, James E. 1966. "Development and Validation of Ego Identity Status." *Journal of Personality and Social Psychology* 3(5):551–558.

_____. 1980. "Identity in Adolescence." In *Handbook of Adolescent Psychology,* edited by Joseph Adelson, 159–187. New York: Wiley.

Phinney, Jean S. 1996. "Understanding Ethnic Diversity." *American Behavioral Scientist.* 40(2):143–152.

Portes, Alejandro, and Rubén G. Rumbaut. 2006. *Immigrant America: A Portrait.* Berkeley: University of California Press.

Ponterotto, Joseph G., and Brent Mallinckrodt. 2007. "Introduction to the Special Section on Racial and Ethnic Identity in Counseling Psychology: Conceptual and Methodological Challenges and Proposed Solutions." *Journal of Counseling Psychology* 54(3):219–223.

Rosenwasser, Penny. 2002. "Exploring Internalized Oppression and Healing Strategies." *New Directions for Adult and Continuing Education* 94(summer):59–62.

Tajfel, Henri. 1978. *The Social Psychology of Minorities.* London: Minority Rights Group.

_____, and John Turner. 1979. "An Integrative Theory of Intergroup Conflict." In *The Social Psychology of Intergroup Relations,* edited by William G. Austin and Stephen Worchel, 94–109. Monterey, CA: Brooks-Cole.

Tamburri, Anthony Julian. 1991. *To Hyphenate or Not to Hyphenate.* Montreal: Guernica.

Twenge, Jean M., and Jennifer Crocker. 2002. "Race and Self-Esteem: Meta-Analyses Comparing Whites, Blacks, Hispanics and American Indians." *Psychological Bulletin* 128(3):371–408.

United States Census Bureau. *American FactFinder 2005–2009.* American Community Survey. Available at http://factfinder.census.gov/servlet/DatasetMainPageServlet?_program=ACS.

Uslaner, Eric. 2008. "Where You Stand Depends on Where Your Grandparents Sat: The Inheritability of Generalized Trust." *Public Opinion Quarterly* 72(4):725–740.

Wakefield, W. David, and Cynthia Hudley. 2007. "Ethnic and Racial Identity and Adolescent Well-being." *Theory into Practice* 46(2):147–154.

Waterman, Alan S. 1982. "Identity Development from Adolescence to Adulthood: An Extension of Theory and a Review of Research." *Developmental Psychology* 18(3):341–358.

Wester, Stephen R., Daniel L. Vogel, Wei Meifen, and Rodney McLain. 2006. "African American Men, Gender Role Conflict, and Psychological Distress: The Role of Racial Identity." *Journal of Counseling and Development* 84(4):419–429.

What Am I? Where Is My Home? Cultural Identity and Belonging in Postwar Italian Immigrants: 1940s to 2002

LUCIA IMBESI

The idea for the small, preliminary study described in this essay came to me after listening on the radio and TV to two men describing their feelings about living in a foreign country. One was an Israeli man of letters, the other an Italian medical researcher. I was struck by the similarity of their narratives. Except for the language difference, the feelings, thoughts, and even the words were remarkably similar; painfully so, because what they did express was a deep pain and loss, an old, chronic, pervasive pain that was with them always. I thought then of the millions of immigrants who leave their homeland and often their loved ones behind. In particular, I asked myself how does the experience of leaving home and being surrounded by a new culture affect their cultural identity? How do they come to think of themselves? What happens to their sense of home and belonging? What kind of adjustment is made?

Cultural identity is a central component of the totality of personal identity, of the whole self. Included in the concept are cultural self-definition, the feeling of likeness to and emotional resonance with a particular group. The sense of belonging and of home may be separate from cultural self-definition but nevertheless intimately tied to it at the same time. LaFromboise, Coleman, and Gerton (1993) define cultural identity as " . . . the evolution of a sense of self in relation to a culture of origin and who one is within and without that cultural context" (402).

A great deal has been written about the phenomenon of immigration and the process of acculturation in the last eighty years. Park (1928) and Stonequist (1935) saw biculturalism as leading to marginalization and consequently to psychological conflict, a divided self and disjointedness. Stonequist (1935) further postulated that such individuals develop a dual pattern of identification, a divided loyalty and ambivalent attitudes as a result of their dual position in the larger culture. Therefore, biculturalism was seen as undesirable psychologically for the individual, though it may benefit society in the long run. Subsequent researchers have disagreed with this "marginal" theory and all its negative implications (Goldberg 1941; Green 1947). Since then, a great many aspects of acculturation and biculturalism have been researched. For our purposes, we will limit ourselves to issues of cultural identity and/or the sense of home and belonging. There seems to be wide consensus in the literature that the ability to integrate the original culture with the new, larger culture ensures the best results in the process of acculturation [see LaFromboise, Coleman, and Gerton (1993) for a review]. Phinney (1990) points out that immigrants may maintain separate, independent identifications in relation to their mother culture and to their newly adopted one (a bidimensional perspective). Integration rather than assimilation is widely considered more desirable than assimilation (commonly known as the melting pot). A social network made up of both old and new cultures provides "groundedness" and ensures mental health (LaFromboise, Coleman, and Gerton 1993):

> Being grounded in both cultures will allow the individual to both maintain and enhance his or her personal and cultural identities in a manner that will enable him or her to effectively manage the challenges of a bicultural existence. (408)

Berry, a pioneer in this field of study, has published extensively on issues of acculturation, identity, and adaptation (Berry 1997, 2005; Berry et al. 2006; see also Ward 2008). Berry (1997) postulated four modes of acculturation: (1) Assimilation, in which there is little interest in cultural maintenance and interaction with the larger society is preferred; (2) separation, where old cultural affiliation is sought and contact with the new is avoided; (3) marginalization, in which neither cultural maintenance nor contact with the larger society is maintained; and (4) integration, which consists of both cultural maintenance and involvement with the new larger society. In their studies on acculturation and adaptation, Berry (1997, 2005) and Berry et al. (2006) also found that immigrants who integrated, rather than assimilated, showed much better adaptation socially and psychologically. Interestingly, in their 2006 study with teenage immigrants, Berry and co-workers found an unexpected percentage fell in the conflicted/problematic category. These young people appeared to be marginal and confused. Ward (2008) focused on the study of conflict arising from immigration and concluded that for some individuals traditional versus new identifications (depending on how different they may be from each other) may be experienced as incompatible and conflict may be engendered by irreconcilable identities.

The history of Italian American immigrants' ethnic identity is particularly interesting as it is tied not only to the vicissitudes of immigration and all that the Italians encountered in the New World but also to Italy's own history as a nation, that is, Italy's belated unification (Luconi 2007, 2011). At the turn of the twentieth century, the Italian immigrant's national identity as "Italian" had been postulated as practically nonexistent. The acquisition of "Italianness" arose out of their experience as immigrants. Ethnic attachment to the mother country was strongly regional and local (known as *campanilismo* in Italy). In fact, community enclaves consisting of immigrants from a particular town or region (or even small village) formed in the varied cities where they settled. Such subnational divisions were even found in mutual aid and fraternal associations, which limited membership only to immigrants from a specific area (Pozzetta 1989; Luconi 2004, 2007, 2011). A national "Italian" identity, therefore, grew over the decades, encouraged by Italy's wartime conquests of Libya in 1912 and the annexation of Ethiopia in 1936 and further strengthened by fascism, which promoted national pride. As Luconi (2007, 2011) pointed out, the consolidation of Italian national identity and pride was also a significant defensive reaction to anti-Italianism and discrimination.

As Pozzetta's (1989) comprehensive historiography has pointed out, since the dimension of ethnicity became an accepted category for historical analysis, Italian Americans as immigrants and as an ethnic group have received extensive study, including internationally. Many aspects have been studied including discrimination and the role of shame. However, social science literature has been divided with regard to the strength of ethnic identity. Some social scientists contend that there is a decline with each generation, while others point to a resurgence of ethnic consciousness. Roche's 1982 study of three generations of Italian Americans in the suburbs of Rhode Island found a lessening of ethnic behavior and attachment with each generation. The results of that study supported assimilation theories. Pozzetta (1989) also pointed to the split in the literature with regard to Italian Americans' retention of their ethnicity, citing authors such as Richard Alba and James Crispino who contend that ethnicity is not a strong force. Sala, Dandy, and Rapley (2010) explored the construction of identity in a small sample of bilingual Italian Americans in Australia. These authors found Italian identification to be a multiple, fluid, and negotiable category, marked by language, biological heritage, and the group's practices related to food. Identifications were not clear-cut, stable, or unitary. On the other hand, Ferraiuolo (2006), in his study of Italian Americans in Boston's North End, pointed to the immigrants' manipulation of symbols in the form of the Italian language and especially the use of dialect to convey kinship and their Italian group identity, then switching to English to demonstrate their negotiation of a new American identity as appropriate to circumstances. An even more important symbol was the celebration of religious feast days to evoke their local cultural Italian origins (the hometown). The use of the religious festive system was the main symbol used to negotiate their Italian identity.

In looking at data, and especially during interviews, this author sought answers to the following questions: (1) How did respondents identify culturally following immigration? (2) To what extent are old identifications held? (3) What factors may promote the formation of new identifications? (4) What happens to the sense of home and belonging? (5) How much resolution is there?

METHODOLOGY

A questionnaire consisting of fifty-four items, in both Italian and English, was devised and utilized. Most respondents preferred the Italian version. Respondents were encouraged to elaborate as much as possible. The sample consisted of persons who emigrated after World War II up to 2002. Only respondents who had been residing in the United States at least eight years were included. Items consisted of: (a) Demographic data, including level of education and home ownership; (b) social involvement with both cultures; (c) cultural identifications, that is, self-definition, values, affinity in thought and emotions, observed customs; and (d) the sense of home and belonging. Questions asked were the same for both Italy and America. Following are some sample items from the questionnaire:

ITEM 30: I consider myself: (a) American (b) Italian (c) Other ____.
ITEM 31: My home is: (a) America (b) Italy (c) Other ____.
ITEM 35: In my way of thinking I am most like: (a) the Americans (b) the Italians (c) Other ____.

ITEM 37: The people who feel most familiar and see myself in them are: (a) American (b) Italian.

ITEM 39: When people speak about "home," I immediately think _____. Please explain/elaborate.

ITEM 42: When I'm in Italy I feel like: (a) I belong (b) that I don't quite belong (c) Other ____.

ITEM 51: When I am in Italy with a group of locals I feel: (a) right at home (b) like a stranger (c) different (d) just like them (e) none of these.

Seventy-two questionnaires were received, mostly from the New York metropolitan area, New Jersey, and Long Island. Responses were also solicited through an article published in *America Oggi*. Twenty-six follow-up interviews were conducted by this author. Many respondents could not be contacted as they did not provide contact information, and some did not wish to be interviewed because of time pressures. (For additional data, please see the appendices at the end of the essay).

In determining identity, answers to Item 30 were decisive. However, it should be noted that answers to this item were often contradicted by answers to subsequent questions such as Item 34. Item 30 was chosen as most definitive because this author believes that it may represent the most "conscious" of respondents' feelings/sense of self/choice pertaining to identity. Also, because it is the first such question, it may reflect immediacy or coming from the "gut." Similarly, Item 31 was used to determine definition of "home."

Follow-up interviews were semistructured (see Appendix D) and lasted from one-half hour to one hour. Many were conducted in person by this author, some on the phone; manual notes were taken.

IDENTITY

I would like to emphasize that for the concepts of identity and home there were a great many contradictions in respondents' answers. Even in those cases where identity and/or home were strongly and clearly held verbally during interviews, written answers showed many contradictions.

Overall, thirty-eight percent of respondents identified as Italian, nineteen percent as American, thirty-three percent as Italian and American (or, as some specified: "Hybrid"), and seven percent did not define their identity. It is notable that several respondents, mostly professionals, spontaneously identified themselves as Italian when it came to their emotional, cultural selves but emphasized that they are American when it comes to their professional and practical functioning. For this group, the whole concept of work revealed itself to be a significant component in terms of cultural identity. In addition, even those who identified as American often stated that they felt closest emotionally to other Italians. Those who identified themselves as Italian American or "hybrids" often cited personal taste preferences such as food, fashion, emotionality, and values such as the family as Italian, while their practical functioning and work ethic were defined as their American selves. Some distinguished between being Italian American and Italian and American. These respondents saw as Italian American only those of Italian ancestry, but born in the United States, and believed that the cultural difference is a distinguishing factor, and saw them as a distinct group and different from themselves. Most respondents had a good deal of contact with Italy and, to a lesser extent, other Italian immigrants.

HOME AND BELONGING

Fifty-eight percent of respondents identified America as home, eighteen percent identified Italy as their home, and seven percent identified both countries as home. Sixteen percent could not define home or were conflicted. As we can see, the percentage identifying America as home is quite significant. However, though many chose one or the other as home on paper, on specific questions about belonging, at least twenty percent felt they did not have a feeling of belonging to either country. Many of these could not be reached for an interview. Of those who were interviewed, some felt that they did not know where their home was, that they lost their home by immigrating, or that they felt like they were divided between the two countries and could not choose one or the other; they had one foot here and one foot there. As stated earlier, answers to both cultural identity and home and belonging were far from straightforward or consistent, with a great many contradictions. For example, a respondent might identify as Italian, but then say he/she is most like the Americans. Many identified America as home, but in answer to the question "When people speak about 'home' I immediately think_____," many people filled in their childhood home, their home in Italy. Similarly, many people identified America as their home but stated that their hearts are in Italy. For many who answered "America" as their home, the criteria used by them was often the physical place. In fact, a number of them gave New York specifically as their home and felt no affinity for, or identification with, the rest of the United States as their home. The world outside New York was seen as foreign. Interestingly, this was true of some of the more educated respondents. With few exceptions, respondents who had immigrated more than twenty-five years ago identified America as home. Family and length of time in the United States were often cited as being crucial determinants in their identification of home, even those who held a strong Italian identity. Some qualified their answers by saying that America is their physical home, but Italy is their emotional home. The concept of home and belonging seemed to be much more conflictual and ambiguous than that of identity. For example, a person might state that Italy is his/her home but that he/ she doesn't have a feeling of belonging when there. Others may feel that America is their home but they don't have a feeling of belonging totally in the United States. Respondents were often unable to explain these contradictions. Therefore, there appeared to be confusion about identity, but more so in the case of home and belonging. Although it was evident to this author that there was confusion, most of the respondents chose one or the other and did not necessarily experience the confusion or conflict consciously. Again, in their identifications, the existence of family in America, the length of time since they arrived, and the emotional quality of their lives were crucial determinants (i.e., even those who expressed some conscious regret, longing, or conflict about emigrating stated that they were not unhappy but, rather, were generally content with their lives). The overwhelming majority of respondents felt that emigrating was something they would recommend—what they gained, besides possible economic opportunities, is a freeing up of their selves, an enrichment of their experiences, and a greater understanding of the world. This was so even among respondents who were conflicted or downright negative about living in America. It is to be noted that this small sample of respondents was very varied in terms of socioeconomic background and education, and I believe that those factors may also be significant in terms of identity and belonging. This is exemplified by the following group of respondents.

THE LOYAL TO AMERICA GROUP

The Loyal to America group was made up mostly of immigrants who came in the late 1940s and 1950s, many from Sicily, who were married with children. These respondents identified themselves as American and considered America to be their home. However, closer examination revealed that they have almost no dealings with American people or American culture in general, have not traveled around the United States, socialize almost exclusively with family members and people from their hometowns in Italy, frequent their towns' social clubs, and are, in general, very divorced from American life, outside of what they view on TV. Many of them read the Italian American newspaper and watch RAI International. One might say that they have successfully re-created in America the small-town life and milieu they left behind. When asked what makes them American, they often talked about the concrete aspects of America that they like, comparing them to the inefficiencies of Italian systems. They could not identify aspects of their personalities, values, mode of functioning, thinking, or feeling that makes them American, except in some very vague way that they could not put into words. However, they felt and saw themselves as unmistakably American and identified with America and everything for which it stands. This group expressed a very strong sense of loyalty toward America. I wondered whether such identification might be motivated by a rejection of their modest origins. Almost all were blue-collar, although not poor when they emigrated (only two of the respondents came from a poor, farming background). My conjecture about rejecting their socioeconomic roots was wrong. Almost all invariably reported beautiful and pleasurable memories of Italy. Almost all continue to visit Italy and maintain very regular contacts with family and friends there but see themselves as "different" from the people in their hometowns. I even ventured to ask a few of these people whether they had ever felt ashamed of being Italian. The answer was a decisive "no." They also were very clear that they did not long to live in Italy ever again. One of these respondents expressed anger at the fact that Italy did not provide the conditions necessary to continue living there and also stated that if conditions in Italy had been what they are today, she would not have left. This respondent described her life in America as "hard." Another respondent, a man who fit the above description, stated that if he had to do it over, he would not choose to emigrate. There were many other stories of initial hardship. However, most in this group had done reasonably well economically, and most owned their own homes. For most, there was a sense of having gained by coming to the United States and that, therefore, America should come first for them. The members of this group were the most consistent in their identity and sense of belonging even during interviews. When pressed, one of them stated, "Dove c'é il letto, c'é il rispetto;" an old saying that translates as "Respect the host that gives you a bed." Therefore, loyalty emerged as a significant factor in these immigrants' identifications. This group was the most "resolved."

Those respondents who identified as Italian often spontaneously stated that they were proud to be Italian. Though shame was not specifically investigated in this study, respondents' answers and narratives about Italy or their identity did not reflect any disavowal or shame, such as Caputo (2011) has written about. However, these same respondents often chose to identify America as their home and expressed loyalty and appreciation for America and the things America had given them. Loyalty and gratitude toward America, length of time, and family were cited as factors. Again, expressed memories and images of Italy were very positive. There were a couple of exceptions among the newer immigrants. These were young people, mostly in their thirties, who were very critical of Italy and Italian society, the political system there, and the system of nepotism, which stifles equal economic opportunity, in particular.

THE CONFLICTED OR UNRESOLVED GROUP

Another group that caught my attention was the one that I labeled "conflicted" or "unresolved." The criteria used for this category was the presence of one or more of the following: (1) The conscious feeling of not really having a home; (2) conscious doubt as to either identity or home and belonging; (3) uncertainty about remaining in the United States; and (4) a certain amount of conscious psychological discomfort with regard to home and/or identity. The total number in this group was eighteen. This number might be somewhat larger since some respondents left the question of home blank. They could not be contacted for clarification. These respondents also felt "different" from both Italians and Americans. Most saw Italy as their home, but their sense of home and belonging was compromised. They could best be described as having "one foot in Italy and one in America," at least emotionally, and, sometimes, literally.

Home ownership was less frequent in this group and one respondent stated that her conflict about home was the reason she would not buy property in this country. One person described it as living in "limbo." Many, but not all, expressed the desire to live in Italy, or in both countries, in their old age. All have had intense involvement with Italy and other Italians. Eleven came from the north of Italy, seven from the south. Most had a university degree. Ages ranged from thirties to seventies, with the greatest number in their thirties. Eleven identified as Italian, five as Italian and American, and none as American. There was variation as to length of time in the United States; however, the greatest percentage, fifty-five percent, emigrated in the last fifteen years. Only eight out of eighteen were married with children. Three of these, married with children, thought they might go back to live in Italy again. Of particular interest were those who came to this country as children. The total number of these was three, one male and two females. Although most of their lives have been spent in the United States, their hearts were divided, and they often felt that they had lost their homes. Here, too, their sense of home and belonging was much more compromised than their sense of identity. In contrast to the rest of the unresolved group, these three would not recommend emigrating. This author postulates that the fact that they came as children brought by their parents and, therefore, not by choice, may be a significant factor in their negative outlook on emigrating. However, this is not conclusive as there were other respondents who came as children but did not have the same conflicted or negative feelings.

Interestingly, even those respondents who felt ambivalent toward or downright disliked living in the United States felt that emigrating was worthwhile for them and that they would recommend it. This was true of the great majority of all respondents. Please note that, although they may have been conflicted or unresolved, they were not necessarily unhappy, except for a very small number of respondents. There were only a very few who felt the same kind of pain expressed by the two men who inspired this study (cited at the beginning of this essay). One respondent stands out in particular. He had been in this country for more than forty years, was married with children and grandchildren, and expressed enormous regret at having emigrated, citing many experiences of discrimination and vilification here in America. Discrimination was not explored in this study and this respondent was the only one who spontaneously brought it up.

On the other hand, he was also disappointed with modern-day Italy and was objectively critical of it. It should be noted that several of the conflicted group were in the mental health field. Also, these respondents often came from cities rather than small towns.

DIFFERENT FROM BOTH ITALIAN AND AMERICANS/DON'T BELONG TOTALLY TO EITHER GROUP

Feeling different from both Italians and Americans, as well as the feeling of not totally belonging to either country, was reported also by some who were not consciously conflicted. One respondent who felt very resolved, but different, explained it thus: "I have my Italy inside me; I have my Italy here with me. I don't feel I have lost my Italy." As to the feeling of difference from both, he stated: "Mi sento diverso [dagli italiani], ma della stessa pasta; non so se piú cotto o piú crudo." "I feel different [from the Italians], but of the same dough; I don't know if more cooked or less cooked." This man is surrounded by all that is Italian in America in his daily life and in his work, and I believe that may be crucial to his ability to internalize the lost love object, Italy. Similarly, a young woman, who had been in this country only ten years and identified with both cultures, identified America as her home but also felt different from both Americans and Italians. This young woman resolved the issue of identity and home by re-creating in her New York apartment the elements of her old home and life in Italy (i.e., by consciously surrounding herself with physical and cultural artifacts that she grew up with, beginning with an espresso coffee maker). We can see this as another way to integrate and internalize one's original home, thereby warding off a painful and total sense of loss. This, of course, is a common and universal mode of taking home with us everywhere we go, similar to the way we try to resolve grief following the death of a loved one.

NORTH VERSUS SOUTH

There appeared to be a difference in terms of identity and home between north and south (see Appendix C for statistics). Thirteen out of twenty-four northerners identified as Italian, compared to eighteen out of forty-five southerners. Only two northerners identified as American, but one qualified it in terms of being American because of the number of years living in the country and because her family is in America. However, she added that she, the person, is Italian. The other northerner, who identified as "American" and America as her home, expressed a great deal of rage toward Italy, rejecting all for which Italy stands. Eight, or thirty-three percent, of northerners identified as Italian American and had a feeling of comfort and belonging in both places. One northerner could not identify at all. Northern respondents retained their identity as Italian in higher percentages than southerners, even those who have been in America longer than twenty-five years and whose socioeconomic background was blue collar. Also, northerners were much more critical of both America and Italy in their narratives. However, since the total number of northern respondents was smaller, and since the average length of time in the United States for them was shorter, conclusions about differences between north and south cannot be made at this time. Also, a greater number of northern respondents came from cities, as opposed to small towns or rural areas, and this may play a significant part in identity and sense of belonging. This needs to be studied further.

IDEALIZATION OF ITALY?

With few exceptions, per the questionnaires, most respondents rated their memories of Italy, including childhood memories, as "Beautiful/ Pleasurable." On a scale from one to ten, the average rating for Italy was nine. The average rating for America was seven. During interviews, feelings about Italy were also positive for the great majority of respondents. This may suggest a process of idealization of Italy, as there often is with lost love objects. However, to date, the majority of respondents felt emigrating was worth it and would not return to Italy to live. Also, the overwhelming majority of respondents, with some exceptions, reported their lives in America as "happy" and, during interviews, expressed serenity and contentment about living abroad. When they admitted to missing Italy, it was mostly family and friends that they missed, not the country. This last finding supports some authors' contentions that Italian immigrants do not have strong national ties to their country of origin (Luconi 2011).

DISCUSSION

In analyzing the results of this study, the most obvious implication is how psychologically complex cultural identity and the concept of home seems to be. The extent of contradictions expressed, especially in answers to the questionnaire, points to the existence of all sorts of conscious and unconscious factors at play in cultural identity formation and the sense of belonging. Contradictions also expressed themselves in some respondents' conscious identifications and their actual lifestyles and involvement with the larger society, as in the Loyal to America group. However, the majority of respondents did not seem to experience or express much cognitive dissonance or emotional turmoil in spite of the contradictions. The results of this study suggest that for most of the respondents the presence of family in the United States, home ownership, and length of time in the United States were crucial in determining identifications and enabling emotional resolution. Family, above all, was the determining factor in the sense of home and belonging. This author also believes that since conflict and uncertainty are hard to bear, we can postulate that all sorts of psychological defensive mechanisms might be at play to resolve conflict. This, however, cannot be established from this study and would need additional investigation. It is interesting, however, that the respondents who were most consciously conflicted or emotionally unresolved about both identity and home were in the field of mental health. This suggests the possibility that greater psychological insight may lead to greater doubt and questioning. This, again, is only my own surmising.

LIMITATIONS

The size of the sample is small and mostly limited to a small geographic area, that is, the New York metropolitan area and New Jersey. Also, many of the respondents could not be contacted for follow-up interviews. Although many respondents lived in ethnically mixed neighborhoods, many respondents worked in environments populated by other Italians or other immigrants (e.g., restaurants). One could wonder what the impact would be of working and living in a predominantly American environment with little access to Italian American resources. This was one of the causes of unhappiness for one respondent who had relocated from New York to Florida and whose only access to Italian American culture was *America Oggi*. Issues of discrimination and shame were not explored and, therefore, their influence could not be assessed. Further studies should take into account personal history as well as personality structure.

CONCLUSIONS

It appears from this small, preliminary study that most of the respondents in this sample did not suffer the sort of chronic, painful, almost torturous, loss and longing that the two men who inspired this study experienced. Although cultural and home identifications were full of contradictions, respondents appeared to be resolved as to their identities, for the most part. Cultural identity seemed to be much less conflictual than the sense of home and belonging. This was so even in the most recent immigrants. It appears that the sense of home is most vulnerable to change and is more easily destabilized. One respondent, who was not included in the study because he had only been in the United States for three years, stated that he no longer felt he had a home and did not know where his home was. A longitudinal study might be useful in this respect.

In this study, Italians who emigrated to America after World War II to 2002 have, for the most part, made a successful adjustment to living in the United States. A significant percentage retained their Italian identity or formed a new integrated identity as Italian and American. Cultural identity seemed to be fluid for many, and work ethic emerged as a lesser, but important, determinant, especially for professionals. A smaller, but also significant, percentage formed an exclusively new identity as American. Loyalty to the host country emerged as a significant factor in identity formation. A much greater percentage accepted America as their new home. The presence of family in the United States was the strongest determinant, followed by length of time.

There appeared to be a difference between north and south as to identity and the sense of home. Northerners, even those living in the United States over twenty-five years, tended to retain their Italian identity to a greater extent and to consider Italy as home, as compared wtih southerners. However, this was a much smaller group and the differences need to be studied further.

Those respondents categorized as "conflicted" tended to retain their identity as Italian, and their sense of home and belonging was compromised, causing conscious discomfort, a sense of being in limbo or stranded, in some, but not all. This group was mixed in terms of length of time in the United States and in terms of marital status. It was most interesting to this author that some of the most conflicted were married with children and had been in the United States for more than forty years, while a few came to the United States as children. One wonders, then, about the influence of personality development and personal history. This aspect is worthy of further study.

Finally, almost all respondents kept very close ties to the mother country, expressing almost unanimous positive feelings about Italy. At the same time, a very high percentage of respondents felt that emigrating to America was an experience worth having.

References

Berry, John W. 1997. "Immigration, Acculturation and Adaptation." *Applied Psychology: An International Review* 46:5–68.

_____. 2005. "Acculturation: Living Successfully in Two Cultures." *Intercultural Relations* 29:697–712.

_____, Jean S. Phinney, David L. Sam, and Paul Vedder. 2006. "Immigrant Youth: Acculturation, Identity and Adaptation." *Applied Psychology: An International Review* 55(3):303–332.

Caputo, Lorraine. 2011."Gender, Food and Loss." *Studies in Gender and Sexuality* 12(3):179–195.

Ferraiuolo, Augusto. 2006. "Boston's North-End." *Western Folklore* 65(3) (Summer):263–302.

Goldberg, Milton M. 1941. "A Qualification of the Marginal Man Theory." *American Sociological Review* 1:52–58.

Green, Arnold W. 1947. "A Re-Examination of the Marginal Man Concept." *Social Forces* 26:167–171.

LaFromboise, Teresa, Hardin L. K. Coleman, and Jennifer Gerton. 1993. "Psychological Impact of Biculturalism: Evidence and Theory." *Psychological Bulletin* 114(3):395–412.

Luconi, Stefano. 2004. "Becoming Italian in the U.S.: Through the Lens of Life Narratives." *MELUS* 29(3/4) (Fall/Winter):151–164.

_____. 2007. "The Impact of Italy's Twentieth Century Wars on Italian American Ethnic Identity." *Nationalism & Ethnic Politics* 13(3) (Fall):465–491.

_____. 2011. "Discrimination and Identity Construction: The Case of Italian Immigrants and their Offspring in the USA." *Journal of Intercultural Studies* 32(3):293–307.

Park, Robert E. 1928. "Human Migration and the Marginal Man." *American Journal of Sociology* 5:881–893.

Phinney, Jean S. 1990. "Ethnic Identity in Adolescents and Adults: A Review of Research." *Psychological Bulletin* 108:499–514.

Pozzetta, George E. 1989. "Immigrants and Ethnics: The State of Italian-American Historiography." *Journal of American Ethnic History* 9(1) (Fall):67–95.

Roche, Patrick J. 1982. "Suburban Ethnicity: Ethnic Attitudes and Behavior Among Italian Americans in Two Suburban Communities." *Social Science Quarterly* 63(1)(March):145–153.

Sala, Emanuela, Justine Dandy, and Mark Rapley 2010. "'Real Italians and Wogs': The Discursive Construction of Italian Identity Among First Generation Italian Immigrants in Western Australia." *Journal of Applied Social Psychology* 20(2):110–124.

Stonequist, Everett V. 1935. "The Problem of Marginal Man." *American Journal of Sociology* 7:1–12.

Ward, Colleen. 2008. "Thinking Outside the Berry Boxes: New Perspectives on Identity, Acculturation and International Relations." *International Journal of Intercultural Relations* 32:105–114.

APPENDIX A

DESCRIPTION OF SAMPLE

TOTAL NUMBER OF QUESTIONNAIRES	72
Total Number of Interviews	26
Number of Females	38
Number of Males	34
Age Range	30s to 80s

DISTRIBUTION BY DATE OF IMMIGRATION	
Late 1940s	2
1950s	18
1960s	12
1970s	9
1980s	10
1990s	15
2000–2002	6

MARITAL STATUS	
Married with children	39
Married with no children	3
Divorced with children	11
Single with no children	17
No response	2

GEOGRAPHIC ORIGINS IN ITALY	
North	24
Central Italy	3
South	45

EDUCATIONAL LEVEL	
Elementary School	6
Junior High School	15
High School	17
University	34

APPENDIX B

CULTURAL IDENTITY AND HOME

IDENTITY	
Italian	27 (38%)
Italian/European	2 (03%)
American	14 (19%)
Italian and American	24 (33%)
No response	5 (07%)

IDENTIFICATION OF HOME	
America	42 (58%)
Italy	13 (18%)
Both Italy and America	5 (07%)
Could not define or conflicted	6 (08%)
No response	6 (08%)

MY HEART IS IN	
America	27 (38%)
Italy	28 (39%)
Both	12 (17%)
No response	5 (07%)

APPENDIX C

IDENTITY/HOME BY GEOGRAPHIC ORIGIN

SOUTH OF ROME: No. of Respondents	45
IDENTITY	
Italian	17 (38%)
American	10 (22%)
Italian and American	16 (35.5%)
No response	2 (04%)
IDENTIFICATION OF HOME	
Italy	3 (07%)
America	30 (67%)
Both Italy and America	6 (13%)
No response	6 (13%)

CENTRAL ITALY: No. of Respondents	3
IDENTITY	
American	2 (66.6%)
Italian American	1 (33.3%)
IDENTIFICATION OF HOME	
America	3 (100%)

NORTH OF ROME: No. of Respondents	24
IDENTITY	
Italian	13 (54%)
American	2 (08%)
Italian and American	8 (33%)
No response	1 (04%)
IDENTIFICATION OF HOME	
Italy	9 (37.5%)
America	9 (37.5%)
Both Italy and America	3 (13%)
Could not define or conflicted	1 (04%)
No response	2 (08%)

APPENDIX D

GUIDELINES FOR INTERVIEW

1. How did you feel when you learned that you were coming to live in America and had to leave Italy?

2. How did you imagine America to be?

3. When you arrived in America how was it for you? What did you think? What did you feel?

4. Do you miss Italy now? How much? Do you think about it often?

5. In your daily life how big a part of your mental life is Italy and your Italian identity?

6. You wrote that you consider yourself (Italian/American, etc.) What makes you (Italian; American, etc)?

7. You wrote that your home is _____. How did you come to that?

8. You say that you can be understood best by _____. Tell me about that. What do they understand that (the Americans/Italians) cannot?

9. Do you like Italians in general? Americans? What do you think of them?

10. When you think about Italy, what kind of feeling do you get?

11. In general, in terms of your emotional comfort level, how comfortable is it for you to live in a foreign country (serene, resolved, conflicted)?

12. If you had to do it all over again, knowing what you know now, would you emigrate to America?

13. How does having one foot here and one foot there affect your life? Your decisions? Your choices? (Optional for people who appear to have one foot here and one foot there)

PART TWO

Personal Experiences in Therapy

Recovery is Within Reach

CHRISTINA BRUNI

My break was sudden, total, and irreversible. I had graduated college in June 1987 and I was twenty-two years old. I had a breakdown on a Friday night, and that Saturday morning at ten o'clock I got in the car and my mother drove me to the hospital.

I was first hospitalized in the fall of 1987. That Christmas Eve, the Night of the Seven Fishes, and Christmas day our family celebrated together. I don't know what my cousins were told or if they knew. My brother and twin aunts (my mother's sisters) came to visit me in the hospital.

My beloved Grandpa was in a coma, hooked up to a respirator in the intensive care unit at Victory Memorial Hospital in Brooklyn. That was my breaking point. He died while I was in the hospital, and I didn't go to the funeral. Years later, I wondered what people thought when I wasn't there.

I was in the hospital for three weeks, and within that time, the positive symptoms I exhibited—the paranoia and delusions—disappeared. I've been in remission for more than twenty years. I'm in remission because for over nineteen years I've taken medication every day as prescribed and missed only one dose on the day I had to get a medical test.

The reason I recovered is that my mother drove me to the hospital within twenty-four hours of my breakdown, and I got the right help, right away. She knew something was wrong and got me help; she didn't care how it looked. That is why I recovered. Her one courageous act made all the difference.

A recent survey by the National Alliance on Mental Illness (NAMI) indicates there is an average delay of eight and one-half years between first getting symptoms of schizophrenia and actually being treated (NAMI 2008). The longer you wait to get treatment, the worse the outcome.

As explained in a Harvard Mental Health Newsletter (2008): "Consensus is growing that this first psychotic episode represents a critical period for treating schizophrenia. It offers a unique opportunity to build a therapeutic alliance between patient and clinician, get treatment 'right' the first time around, and do everything possible to improve long-term outcomes." The duration of untreated psychosis, "not only predicts initial treatment response in patients with schizophrenia, but may also affect long-term outcomes." A meta-analysis of 43 studies concluded that "the less time psychosis goes untreated, the more likely that antipsychotics would produce a response, including relief from positive symptoms like hallucinations and negative symptoms like social withdrawal" (1).

The director of the ward told my mother and father, in private, "Mr. and Mrs. Bruni, she won't be able to take care of herself; she knows nothing about her life, and she won't be able to function in this world." The director said I really had to be on medication, and he talked to them nicely, and it made sense to them. "She can't live like this. It's worth trying medication."

Three weeks later, I was released and went back home. A week after that, I started attending a day program, where I met with other people with mental health diagnoses, to attend group therapy, art therapy, ceramics, and individual sessions with a counselor. A year later, I moved into a halfway house and lived there and in supportive living for just over two years.

After I got out of the hospital, I met with a psychiatrist privately and he treated me for eleven years until he died of a heart attack. For close to five years, I also met weekly with an Italian American therapist who had a private practice. His approach was to help me work on the goals I set: To find a full-time professional job and move into my own apartment.

He and I talked about my ethnicity. In all the time I've been in recovery, no other provider ever asked me about the role my heritage might play in my treatment. About seven years ago I saw a male therapist in my neighborhood for about three years. I met a year ago with a female therapist for an intake, and we agreed I could decide whether I wanted to see her because she felt I was doing well enough that I didn't need therapy.

Everyone in my family knows about my illness and they are okay with this, mostly because my mom gives everyone the articles I've written. Even her cousin knows. An interesting thing is that last year I was on Forty-Ninth Street in New York City and I heard the name Chris, and I turned to see that it was my cousin. He was on his dinner break from his job. He asked me what I was doing there, and I said I was seeing my doctor. Since I live in Brooklyn, he thought it odd that I saw a doctor in the City, so I clarified that I was seeing my psychiatrist.

As an Italian American woman, I credit my heritage for helping me recover. In June 2000, I ventured alone to the Cornelia Street Cafe to attend the Italian American Writers Association's (IAWA) monthly poetry reading. Later, in 2004, I was a featured writer, and read from my memoir, *Left of the Dial*. My literary agent, Amanda, is shopping this manuscript, as well as a mental health self-help guide (*Live Life Well*) to editors. My story is a truly hopeful account because I do not have the usual hard luck story: Repeated hospitalizations, drug holidays, and failed treatment. I was hospitalized for a total of only five weeks.

Through IAWA, I met people who knew about my mental health diagnosis and welcomed me with open arms. The Italian American community has been one of my biggest supporters in my efforts to dispel the stigma against people diagnosed with schizophrenia and other mental illnesses. It is a stigma so great that too often it prevents people from seeking help or getting help.

Furthermore, my Italian American identity planted the seeds of my recovery. My father was a New York City firefighter who dreamed of owning his own business. He started a garden center out of a two-car garage in the 1970s, and it became one of the largest of its kind. I surely inherited from him this hard work ethic, ambition, and love and respect for family.

Italian Americans have a great deal of which to be proud. If you have schizophrenia or another mental illness, be proud. To quote from "The Ballad of Sacco and Vanzetti, Part Two," "Only silence is shame" (Baez and Morricone 1971, 1978). You have nothing of which you need to be ashamed; you can have a good life.

You might wonder why I disclose so much personal information on my personal website (christinabruni.com), on the website where I am paid (healthcentral.com/schizophrenia), or in talks I give, like the one at the Italian American Mental Health and Wellness Conference held at the Calandra Institute in 2010. I love to do public speaking. I knew by the time I was thirty-five years old that I wanted to spend my life informing the public about mental health issues. Thus, in the Living Life column I write for *SZ* magazine I talk about my experiences in recovery.

I choose to be open and honest because, quite simply, I don't care what other people think. I'm here in this lifetime to help the people God sent me here to help. Nothing would change in society if I lived in hiding the rest of my life. My success would be a hollow victory if I didn't turn around to show people they can recover, too.

Dr. Martin Luther King, Jr. said, "Our lives begin to die the day we become silent on things that matter" (BrainyQuote 2001–2013). It matters to me that people get access to treatment that works. It matters to me that everyone has the ability to reach the recovery stage of their illness.

In one way, writing about my recovery has helped me, too. My recovery took off when I became the writer I always wanted to be. Creating things of beauty to share with others to make them feel good is the best way I know to heal and be whole. As long as I can do this, I'll be okay.

I speak out. I'm a mental health activist because I believe in my vision that people can recover from schizophrenia and other mental illnesses. In addition, the economic cost of untreated mental illnesses is more than $100 billion each year in the United States and the untold cost in wasted lives due to disability is far greater. (Check out http://www.nami.org/template.cfm?section=about_mental_illness for more information on this subject.) I will go to my grave championing the need for immediate intervention with medication and therapy when someone exhibits the symptoms of schizophrenia.

I will tell all of you reading this chapter that you can be successful living with a mental illness. Reject the stigma. The media images of "crazy" people will continue to fuel ignorance and fear in the general public. However, the truth is that the risk of violence in someone with schizophrenia escalates to twenty-eight percent only with a co-occurring substance abuse problem, according to a study conducted by ABC News (2012).

You are not your illness. Remember this: You are not a schizophrenic; you are a person with schizophrenia. You don't have to define yourself by your illness or your symptoms because you are a human being. You have feelings and needs, hopes and dreams, disappointments and achievements just like everyone else. You have a personality and talents all your own, too. You deserve to feel good about yourself, even if you have a diagnosis of schizophrenia.

You might look around and worry people will think you're "crazy" because you have a mental illness. You don't have to tell anyone about your diagnosis unless you want to get more intimate with them, perhaps a potential marriage partner or a close friend you feel you want to risk telling. It's up to you to whom you disclose and when and how much you tell. Gauge how comfortable you feel the other person will be with it. Try talking about a famous person with a diagnosis, like Jane Pauley or Catherine Zeta-Jones, who both have bipolar disorder. See how the person responds to someone else's diagnosis to determine whether you want to tell them about your own diagnosis.

I had no close friends at the time I was diagnosed with schizophrenia, so I had no one to tell. I met a woman at the halfway house who became a good friend of mine. I attended graduate school at Pratt Institute for three years, and I kept it a secret there, too. The closest friends that I made were through my advocacy work. Our diagnoses were the icebreaker; after that you had to prove yourself. I met my best friend five years ago. My friends all have mental health diagnoses. Some have advanced degrees like me, and others collect government disability checks. I've disclosed publicly at the mental health website where I work. I generally don't tell anyone else I meet, though. I recommend you don't tell your employer or your coworkers.

I've been in remission since 1992, when my psychiatrist instituted a drug holiday (a period of time where one stops taking medication) that failed. Within three months, I had to be hospitalized for two weeks and placed back on the medication. I returned to work and everyone treated me like I was covered with spots. I quickly realized that schizophrenia was a real illness, and it wouldn't go away on its own; only the medication would keep the symptoms at bay. I chose recovery because the alternative for me was not an option. Otherwise, I would have to live in hiding the rest of my life, to deny something that was a significant part of my life. Only by accepting the diagnosis was I able to live free of the guilt and shame. The classic quote is, if you name it, you can claim it. Accepting the diagnosis was the way to own my recovery.

I will always be grateful that I was on the lucky end of the luck of the draw; the medication worked on the first try, and I recovered. Recovery is the commonly used term. You can be recovered and not cured; I was not cured. My psychiatrist told me that I'm in remission because I have no symptoms; and I've been in remission for more than 20 years. As long as I take the medication, I have no symptoms and the side effect is livable. You should talk with your psychiatrist about any side effects before discontinuing the medication on your own.

In June 2000, I obtained a Master's Degree in Library and Information Science. I've worked for more than eleven years as a professional librarian. I'm the Health Guide for www.healthcentral.com/schizophrenia, where I've worked for five years. I'm also the Living Life columnist for

SZ magazine. I also do public speaking engagements on recovery.

Aside from taking the drug as prescribed, I go to the gym every week. I love to travel; I've been to Italy, London, San Diego, and Boston. In August 2011, I moved into a one-bedroom co-op.

I recently worked for ten sessions with a therapist who uses cognitive behavioral therapy (CBT), which focuses on thoughts and behaviors. CBT has become increasingly popular for treating people with schizophrenia who have delusions and hallucinations. I often recommend CBT as an option to people who write to the website for which I work. I'm surprised that more people don't take advantage of CBT; it helps you manage your symptoms and achieve balance at work and in relationships. CBT is also a good form of therapy for other mental health disorders, such as obsessive compulsive disorder (OCD), panic disorder, anxiety, bipolar disorder, and posttraumatic stress disorder (PTSD).

If you have a diagnosis, I hope you are inspired by my story to choose recovery or to seek help for yourself or a loved one if you feel something is not right. My advice to you is to set goals for yourself. Taking your medications and staying in treatment will get you to where you want to be. The reality of your changed circumstance might be too painful for you. However, you must confront your pain head-on. The choice is yours: To seek help or not seek help. The choice comes down to this: Do you want to choose recovery or risk total disability? The great majority of those of us who have schizophrenia or another mental illness will need to take some form of medication and stay in treatment for the rest of our lives.

The choice to me was clear in 1992; I chose life with schizophrenia. I've been in recovery for more than twenty-five years. I'll be blunt about this. I won the battle with my mind; I was a winner because I take the medication every day as prescribed. I'm not ashamed to have this diagnosis anymore; I'm proud of how far I've come and I would like to see that other people have an equal opportunity to succeed.

I would ask you several questions. Do you want to be able to function? Do you want to have a relationship? Go to school? Get a job? Do you have hopes, goals, and dreams for yourself? My advice to you is as follows: Take your medications; set goals and work toward them; collaborate with your treatment team; rely on a support network because you can't do it alone; develop coping skills; get at least seven or eight hours of sleep every night; and create a fitness routine you like to do and get physically active every day.

If you are struggling with a street drug or alcohol addiction or de-pendency, I urge you to investigate whether you also have a co-occurring mental illness that you are self-medicating with the drugs or alcohol. A significant number of people with bipolar disorder and schizophrenia have substance abuse problems, especially people with bipolar disorder. The mental health problem could tend to be overlooked in this instance because the focus is on the drugs or alcohol. Any professional should work to determine if a mental health diagnosis is warranted.

I recommend you log on to the NAMI website: www.nami.org. You can educate yourself about your illness, join the dialogue at the message boards, and find resources and information for living well in recovery. NAMI peer support meetings take place in New York City and through-out the United States, and family support groups are also available for those of us who have a loved one with a mental illness. The Mood Disor-ders Support Group (MDSG) has weekly peer support meetings and fam-ily member meetings in Manhattan. Log on to their website at www.mdsg.org.

Health Central also hosts websites: www.healthcentral.com/anxiety is for anxiety and related conditions, www.healthcentral.com/depression is for depression, and www.healthcentral.com/bipolar is for bipolar dis-order. I work for www.healthcentral.com/schizophrenia.

I decided to risk going to work in 1990 when nobody else I knew with a mental illness was employed, and this decision served me well. I was able to feel like I was productive and contributing my talents to society. What allowed me to progress in my treatment was first accepting my di-agnosis and then evolving in the kinds of work I did. Within three years of being diagnosed with schizophrenia I stopped collecting government disability checks, I lived on my own in a studio by the beach, and I had a job as an administrative assistant with employer health benefits. In 1997, I realized, finally, that I wouldn't rise up to be a corporate superstar. So, I left the gray-flannel insurance field for the library field. The job is low-stress and my co-workers are great people.

I would tell anyone with a mental illness to risk finding work, become involved in a relationship, or do any of the other things that people do who don't have a diagnosis tend to do. Staying at home watching TV all day is not healthy. You might be so depressed that you can't get out of bed, and I can understand that. Yet, if you can work at all at a job, do vol-unteer work, or go to school, I recommend that you do so.

The number-one reason I recovered as fully as I have is that I found the jobs I love as a librarian, writer, and activist. Moving into an advocate's role also helped me because I feel good that I can inspire people to take control and live well in their recovery, too. Taking the medication allows me to be in control. Another positive thing was that I started seeing a new psychiatrist in 2003 who treats me like a human being and believes his patients can recover. I trust him completely. My first psychiatrist was like a friend. The middle psychiatrist I saw for five years tried to get me to be his girlfriend. He was unprofessional and kept trying to get me to switch the medication when I was perfectly fine and had no symptoms. He kept asking me over and over if I was in a relationship, as if that was the only valid goal in my recovery. So, one night I left his office and didn't return. That's when I started seeing the current psychiatrist I refer to glowingly. Years ago, I created my own website to provide links to my magazine articles and blog entries, www.christinabruni.com. There you can also listen to an audio file of my featured reading at Bluestockings Bookstore, where I read from my memoir in December 2010. I speak out because the cost of my silence is too high a price to pay—for myself, living in denial and for others in society who could be helped.

I don't talk about my recovery to toot my own horn. I do it to uplift and inspire you on your own road to recovery. Not all of us will become a CEO, like a friend of mine, and that's okay. You don't have to define yourself by your illness nor by your position in society, your job, title, or degree. All that matters is that you can go about your day as comfortably as possible.

My focus is to tell you that the goal is to live the life you love and love the life you live. You might have limitations your illness imposes on you. Develop coping skills because you are the expert on your own recovery. Mourn the past and move forward. Grieving what you lost is a necessary and healthy part of healing the trauma that is your diagnosis. Expect a better tomorrow in a realistic way. Look at the door that has opened instead of looking with regret at the door that closed.

My diagnosis of schizophrenia turned out to be liberating, not a life sentence, when I understood that I could choose to live life on my own terms. The title of my memoir, *Left of the Dial*, refers to my former career as a disc jockey on WSIA (88.9 FM), a radio station that broadcast left of the commercial end of the FM dial.

I espouse the left of the dial philosophy in my own recovery. I've co-opted the term Left of the Dial from the alternative music scene. It's a philosophy where you live life in tune with your nature. You're not afraid to be true to yourself. You're not ashamed to have a diagnosis. You can be who you are in a world where you might face stigma because of the diagnosis. I suggest you not be afraid to be a little different in how you approach brainstorming solutions and techniques that could help you live well. It takes courage to make these changes, and I understand how hard it can be to live with a mental health diagnosis.

Keep the faith. Always be hopeful. I end on this note: Today, more than ever, with the right treatments and support, it is not only possible to recover, it is probable.

References

ABC News. 2012. http://abcnews.go.com/Health/Healthday/story?id=7629820&page=1#.T_4livXNkYI. May 20.

Baez, Joan, and Ennio Morricone. 1971/1978. "The Ballad of Sacco and Vanzetti, Part Two." Edizioni Musicali, RCA, S.p.A. (ASCAP).

BrainyQuote 2001–2013. http://www.brainyquote.com/quotes/quotes/m/martinluth103526.html

Harvard Mental Heath Letter. November 2008. Published by Harvard Medical School, page 1.

National Alliance on Mental Illness (NAMI). 2008. Schizophrenia: Public Attitudes, Personal Needs, Views from People with Schizophrenia, Caregivers, and the General Public, Analysis and Recommendations, online brochure http://www.nami.org/SchizophreniaSurvey/SchizeExecSummary.pdf

Reflections on My Experiences in Logos, 1969–1971

GIL FAGIANI

In November of 1969, at the age of twenty-four, I entered Logos, a therapeutic community (TC) for drug addicts. The first Logos facility was located on East 137th Street and Saint Ann's Avenue, in the heart of what was known as Fort Apache in the South Bronx. Logos had been founded earlier in the summer by former residents of Synanon and Daytop Village, two of the earliest TCs providing treatment for drug addicts. Synanon, founded by Chuck Dederich of Ocean Park, California, in 1958, is generally credited with being the prototype of all such TCs, where clients typically resided for eighteen months to two years (Yablonsky 1965).

It is important to remember that before the advent of Synanon, drug addiction was considered to be an incurable condition. Certainly the medical establishment had no history of dealing with it successfully. The staff at the early TCs had an implacable hostility toward MDs and "shrinks," deriding them as pill pushers and enablers. In the popular mind, addiction was considered a moral disease, and "once a junkie, always a junkie."

My mother was utterly devastated when she learned of my addiction. She had grown up in Greenwich Village and knew heroin addicts in the 1930s and 40s. She never heard of anyone stopping their drug use except as a result of death or incarceration.

According to Lewis Yablonsky (1986), a sociologist, who was a participant/observer in Synanon, and George De Leon (2000), there are several factors that must exist in order for an organization to be defined as a TC: (1) Voluntary entrance; (2) the use of various group therapy methods, especially the encounter group process; (3) the proper use of addicts as co-therapists; and (4) an open-ended social structure allowing the addict to move up the status ladder into an increasingly responsible position.

While I wasn't mandated by the legal system to go into treatment, I wouldn't have done so if my fiancée hadn't threatened to leave me. Earlier in the year, I had attended an outpatient program called Renaissance in

Westport, Connecticut, but soon dropped out, rationalizing that I couldn't identify with the white upper-class clients. True, I had mostly grown up in suburban Stamford, but my heroin use was limited to Spanish Harlem. The one time I bought heroin from Italians, I narrowly escaped dying from an overdose. These dealers had a direct pipeline to the mafia wholesalers in the old Italian neighborhood along Pleasant Avenue in East Harlem.

What appealed to me about Logos was that I could identify with the mostly black and Puerto Rican clients. I also bonded with the clinical director, Lou Zinzi, an Italian American, who took an avuncular interest in me and approved my admission into the program. Lou had ties to East Harlem: His father owned a junk yard there, and Lou himself had used heroin in the neighborhood. He served as a powerful role model.

An essential part of my healing process was my coming to terms with the estrangement I felt toward my ethnic background. Through my early relationship with Lou and group and individual therapy, I learned to see my father, family, and Italian American upbringing in a more balanced and positive light.

After a few months, I was transferred to a new facility, known as Logos II and housed in a former convent on East 185th Street and Washington Avenue in the Bronx. I was delighted to be a few blocks from the Italian neighborhood of Arthur Avenue, where my paternal grandparents once lived and where my maternal grandmother took me food shopping at the indoor market that Mayor Fiorello La Guardia had ordered built during the Great Depression.

My days at Logos were intense and highly structured, filled with group activities and work details. Crudely stated, two of the central premises of what I will call the old-school TCs were: (1) Addicts are masters of denial and manipulation, and their defense systems need to be demolished by attack therapy; and (2) heroin acts as an anesthetic, and when addicts sober up, they need to be goaded to express long suppressed feelings—or poisons as the TC called them—as an essential part of their healing process.

The goal was to avoid "acting on our feelings," such as giving in to drug cravings and to "manage our feelings" in a way that served our best interest. To use TC jargon, the groups aimed at "putting a callous on our bellies," so that we could learn to deal with life's up and downs without resorting to drugs.

The groups challenged negative behavior and emphasized direct confrontation and uninhibited expression of emotion. Residents were encouraged to "drop slips" on peers if they had feelings toward them. For example, if I was angry at someone for not pulling his or her weight in the kitchen, I could write his or her name on a slip of paper, drop it in a box, and the staff would arrange it so I could confront the person in an encounter group.

Initially, I found the encounter groups too intimidating to say a word. Logos was affiliated with the Department of Psychiatry at Lincoln Hospital and hosted two interns. One of them met with me on an individual basis and helped me to prepare myself for the emotional showdowns that often took place in the group sessions. In time, I learned to give as good as I got. Since Logos was expanding rapidly, I found myself leading groups after my third month in the program.

Logos residents were enrolled in public assistance and donated all benefits to the program. A limited amount of funding came from New York City's Addiction Service Agency. Overall, the program operated on a shoestring. For example, food could be very sparse, and at times a meal consisted of a "therapeutic sandwich:" Peanut butter without jelly. Like other TCs at the time, Logos had an acquisition or hustling team that went out into the community and solicited donations. Often what we brought back determined what we ate for dinner. Members of the acquisition team faced enormous pressure, and coming home empty-handed wasn't an option. I remember once wrangling for a donation with one of the owners of an Italian grocery store on Arthur Avenue, who picked up a heavy can of plum tomatoes and threatened to bounce it off my head if I didn't get out of his face.

The late 1960s and early 1970s were a period of ferment and innovation. Besides encounter groups, I was exposed to a myriad of therapeutic techniques, including gestalt therapy, psychodrama, and marathon groups that lasted up to three days.

Logos emphasized self-control and discipline, and, when residents were found to have violated the rules of the program, they were subjected to—in TC jargon—"a learning experience." These could range from a loss of privileges and status, such as a job demotion, or restriction to more severe sanctions, known as "contracts." Emblematic of the old-school approach were contracts that required residents to have their heads shaved—in the case of women they had their hair stuffed into a stocking cap—and wear signs criticizing their "dopefiend behavior." Having been a cadet at a military college for four years, I had few run-ins with the staff regarding disciplinary issues.

I hadn't been at Logos long when the clinical director, Lou Zinzi, died. As a result, the executive director began to play an increasingly more active role in the program. A bright, but insecure man, who suffered from delusions of grandeur, he decided to change the basic mission of Logos. Like other TCs, the original goal was to cure residents of their addiction and to reintegrate them into society as productive, law-abiding citizens.

Taking his cues from his mentor, Chuck Dederich of Synanon, the executive director decided the new mission of Logos was to become an alternative community, headquartered in a huge upstate facility in Liberty, New York, once the second largest hotel in the Catskills. The concept of reentry back into society was to be replaced by permanent citizenship in a utopian colony.

This fundamental shift in the nature of Logos led to a client rebellion in which I was one of the principal leaders. Months before the rebellion, at the invitation of one of the psychiatric interns, I had joined "Think Lincoln," a group of activist doctors, nurses, and workers that had been battling with New York City for decent medical services and the construction of a new Lincoln Hospital. Since my summer stay in East Harlem in 1966, I identified with the radicals of the New Left, which included Students for a Democratic Society, or SDS, the protest movement against the war in Vietnam, the Black Panthers, and the Young Lords. While in Logos, I steeped myself in contemporary revolutionary literature. In a disturbing coincidence, Carmen Rodriguez, a resident of Logos, died at Lincoln Hospital from malpractice. Her death triggered a takeover of the hospital by a coalition of militant community groups.[1]

After fourteen months in Logos, I left the program in January 1971 and moved into an apartment with my fiancée. Eventually, after about half the residents of Logos departed, we set up an alternative program, called the Spirit of Logos, and fought to be recognized by the Board of Estimate of New York City as the legitimate Logos drug program. Clean from heroin and steeled by my leadership experiences at Logos, I func-

[1]For discussion and analysis of the situation at Lincoln Hospital during the 1960s and early 1970s see Ehrenrich (1971) and "Insitutional Organizing" (1972).

tioned as a professional revolutionary for the next three years; but that is another story.[2]

When I look back on my experiences at Logos, I see them not just through the eyes of an ex-client but through the lens of a substance abuse professional who has directed a TC—albeit a light one—for twenty years. What I appreciated most about Logos was the identification and trust I felt toward staff and residents that allowed me to express and explore feelings I had long bottled up, as well as the opportunity to succeed at various leadership positions. At a time when I suffered from shame and self-loathing, Logos offered me asylum, sanctuary, and a place to regain my self-respect. Finally, Logos helped me toughen myself emotionally. It strengthened me to the point that I was able to endure severe family crises in the future, including dealing with two mentally ill children.

Of course, the old-school approach suffered from many deficiencies. There was little oversight of the staff who exercised an enormous power over a vulnerable population. At times they acted in ways that by today's clinical and ethical standards would be considered abusive.

Some of the so-called "learning experiences" violated a client's dignity and reinforced his or her sense of worthlessness as an addict. Another weakness was the dogmatic rejection of medical and mental health professionals, an alliance that would have fostered a deeper understanding of the clients and the factors sustaining their addiction.

The old TCs—like the rest of society—were ignorant of the dangers that alcohol use presented to recovering drug addicts and believed that some recovering heroin addicts could drink safely. As a result, a significant percentage of TC graduates went on to become alcohol dependent, including myself.

In summary, I believe that Logos may very well have saved me from an early death, as well as helped prepare me to deal with future crises. I also believe a modified TC, with a professionally trained and supervised staff, made up predominately of recovering addicts, remains an effective treatment modality in dealing with addiction.

---

[2] For the political evolution of the Spirit of Logos see Fagiani (1994).

References

De Leon, George. 2000. *The Therapeutic Community: Theory, Model and Method*. New York: Springer.

Ehrenrich, Barbara. 1971. *The American Health Empire: Power, Profits and Politics*. New York: Random House.

Fagiani, Gil. 1994. "An Italian American on the Left: Drugs, Revolution, and Ethnicity in the 1970s." In *Italians in a Multicultural Society*, edited by Jerome Krase and Judith N. DeSena, 217–235. New York: Forum Italicum.

"Institutional Organizing." 1972. *Health PAC Bulletin* No. 37, January. Health/PAC, 47 West 14th Street, 3rd Floor, New York, NY 10011.

Yablonsky, Lewis. 1965. *Synanon: The Tunnel Back*. New York: Macmillan.

_____. 1986. *The Therapeutic Community*. New York: Gardner Press.

Experiences in Therapy

FRED GARDAPHÉ

I knew I was in trouble when I started crying and couldn't stop. I had not cried since the death of my father, more than forty years earlier—that's when my grandfather told me that now I was the man in the family and men don't cry. Those were the last tears I shed until I turned fifty, when my wife announced one night that she was leaving me. That's when I experienced what only now I know was a nervous breakdown.

I had never felt so weak in my life and had no idea why. I couldn't sleep for more than three hours at time—and I had been the kind of person who could fall asleep at any time and in any place. I didn't know what was happening to me; only that I had to seek help. I thought that if I could get myself straightened out my wife would realize she was making a mistake and change her mind. Actually, she was the one who gave me two referrals: One was a psychiatrist and the other a psychologist. I didn't want anything to do with medication, so I chose the psychologist. Over the last few years, I had been slowly peeling away the layers of my protection: Drugs, alcohol, sex, nicotine, caffeine, and food. Finally, all that was left was me and my behavior, me and my past, me and the reasons my wife was leaving me—all things I had to deal with but couldn't. That's when I desperately began a couple of years of treatment that, as I see now, more than seven years later, made me mentally healthy.

I had grown up in an Italian American family, where even the contagiously sick were never left alone. To be alone was a great insult to others in the family. So when I was psychologically sick, which I now realize was most of my life from the age of ten to fifty, the only way I could deal with it was to keep it to myself. There was no one I could talk to about what was bothering me. Even when I realized I was sick, I could not publicly acknowledge this illness. First of all, I had buried all I wanted to say through the tradition of male denial of emotion that had been engrained in me since birth. I refused to recognize that what I had was an illness; the ill were weak, and ever since my father's death, when I was ten years old,

I had to be strong. I was the oldest son and immediately took my father's place at home and at work in my grandfather's pawnshop, the very place where my father was murdered. Having no idea what it meant to be a man, I learned it the way I had learned almost everything else up to that point—I simply began imitating the men in my life. The men I knew smoked, drank, and had sex, so I just did what they did. I was not only allowed to do all of this, but I was also accepted into the ranks of manhood at that early age.

I had dealt with this psychological illness throughout my life through self-medication. My medicine at times was alcohol and drugs—legal and often illegal—work, study, caffeine, food, sex, whatever I could find that would keep me from feeling anything. I was numbed by whatever I could put between me and dealing with the real problems of my life. As I got older, and slowly weaned myself free of dependencies, I felt I was rising from the bottom of a sea, surfacing slowly through layers that had, since the age of ten, protected me and kept me from feeling anything.

The one behavior I did not think of losing was reading. In many ways, reading became a way to arm myself against a world that threatened life and traditional masculinity every day. As the line in the Paul Simon (1965) song goes, "I have my books and my poetry to protect me." Through the acceptable role of intellectual, I learned to build walls between me and whatever I began to feel. I had grown up believing that feelings were for women and actions for men. Thought, while respected, was not as important or practical as actions, but thought could certainly protect me from feeling, so I decided to develop my intellectual capacities as a way of protecting myself.

Early in my intellectual development, I would hide my knowledge from friends and fellow workers who teased me whenever I came back to work after attending classes by calling me "the professor." After all, who was I to lift myself out of mediocrity through education? Did I think that I was better than they, who, without education, were stuck driving trucks and working in warehouses? Once, when I skipped a class and came into work early, an old man I worked with asked me why I had come in so early. I told him I needed the hours and that I wasn't sure that a college education was for me. He told me something that I have never forgotten: "What you carry in your head, you don't have to carry on your back." I went on to a successful career in academia, becoming a professor and author of articles and books.

I was trained to believe that scholars are objective and write from a perspective that does not betray their upbringing, their prejudices, or their personal lives. When I decided to work on a book about the representation of Italian masculinity through the gangster figure, I thought I could put my firsthand knowledge to use without revealing anything about myself. When I first started researching masculinity, I thought there was no one more objective than me. After all, I had read all of the major studies of masculinity and its expression in cultures both American and Italian. I had read all the works on Italian American culture that mattered; so when it came to putting the two together, there was no one better suited for the task than me. I had given a few public presentations on the subject, and I sold this book to a publisher before I had written it. I was on a roll. I wrote two chapters in two months. Then, something happened while I was writing this book that made me begin to rethink the way I was made and the way I had behaved that probably led to my divorce.

When my wife left me, I couldn't think clearly, couldn't write, and worse, I couldn't act—I was frozen. Although, to my knowledge, nothing has yet been written about the role that intellect plays in signifying Italian American masculinity, I can tell from personal experience that the more a man's intelligence is perceived to be academic and not practical (i.e., useful, as in medicine, law, or business), the more suspect a man's masculinity is.

These were some of the things I discussed with my therapist. We met once a week, and I soon learned to talk about what I had never discussed with anyone. My therapist was a woman who said very little. She would sit and listen to me and then guide me along through probing questions. I was getting impatient. I had come for a cure; one that I believed she held in her hands and was not sharing with me. The readings she suggested I devoured and discussed with her. A number of times she made allusions that I thought were wrong. When I corrected her, she pointed out that that was an example of how I used my intellect to skirt the real issues at hand. Accuracy in quotation was besides the point in interpreting what was said. I was paying attention only to surfaces, to reflections of meanings and the gathering of as many meanings as possible, instead of figuring out how to apply that knowledge to my life. My mind was disconnected from my body.

She couldn't match me in personal and intellectual knowledge of Italian American culture, but she was able to learn from me, and my treatment became an exchange of knowledge, a relationship built on human equality. I told her what I had experienced and she helped me see what I had missed along the way in my development. I had never properly grieved the many deaths I had encountered. I felt as though I was emotionally still a ten-year-old child and that, slowly, I was growing up. She taught me how to move away from the physical and intellectual ties I had made in the world and move toward the physical and psychological, confronting for the first time in my life the meaning of the murders of my godfather, my father, and my grandfather.

I had known that my brother, who had actually witnessed my grandfather's murder, had been treated by a psychiatrist and with the help of medication had managed to maintain a relatively calm life. My sister had also told me of her treatment and how her therapist had told her that her life was like *The Godfather* films—something I thought was dismissive, and wondered if he thought her life was like that, what would he say about mine? I had actually spent ten years in that milieu.

I had thought therapy was good for those who were weak, and that strong people like me didn't need help; I could do it all on my own. In spite of how hard I tried to make sense of my life through reading—everything from the classics to social sciences, history, fiction, poetry—whenever I needed help, all I had to do was find the right book and I would be fine. So, that was it. When I started therapy, I told no one in my family for a while. Then, there came a point at which I started telling everyone: Strangers, friends, and family, anyone who would listen. I became like the old sailor in Coleridge's "The Rime of the Ancient Mariner"— a man obsessed with telling his story to others. For the first time in my life, I was able to talk about everything that I had hidden through shame, and that incredible freedom to talk often became an unbearable burden for those who listened; I had no idea how obnoxious I had become until I tried to establish new relationships with women. I was learning that the silence of men was a way to avoid dealing with the problems that were fundamental to developing relationships.

There is an old Italian saying, "Le parole sono femmine, e i fatti sono maschi"(Words belong to women, and actions to men). This philosophy resurfaces every now and then in popular culture, most recently through Tony Soprano (a character on the HBO TV series, *The Sopranos*), who asks his psychiatrist, "What ever happened to Gary Cooper, the strong, silent type?" This notion of manly silence has dominated popular portrayals of men for a long time, so that one's masculinity gets questioned whenever a man expresses how he feels. Realizing this helped me to go on with the writing of my book, and I attribute this to my therapy.

For nearly two years, I met with my therapist once a week. We went through my life, and, in the process, I confronted those things that had kept me from feeling. With her help, I began to not just feel but, for the first time in my life, to understand how to deal with my feelings. I worked my way through the stages of grief. More importantly, I began to understand the role that my mother played in my life. Until therapy, I had believed that she was a saint; someone who had endured tragedies and had risen above them all to take care of her four children. I saw, for the first time, that I was not in this alone, that I had developed a style of life that was in direct contrast to her. She cried; I didn't. She depended on others; I didn't.

I was told that to understand myself I had to understand my origins and that meant getting the stories of my parents, especially my mother. After a few weeks of telling my therapist the stories I had been told, she asked me why, whenever I started talking about my mother, I would shift to my father. I couldn't really answer that. Perhaps, it's because my mother, orphaned at the age of seven and widowed at the age of thirty-five, was a saint; and none of my problems could possibly have been caused by a Saint Anna. What could be wrong? I was the oldest son to an Italian American mother!

After each therapy session, I would take my mother out for lunch and talk. I had to get her out of her kitchen, where she controls everything and can concoct any matter of diversion to avoid doing things she doesn't want to do and saying things she doesn't want to say. If you eat her food, you will do what she tells you. It's that simple. Anyway, it was through these conversations that I learned to pierce the mystique of Italian American motherhood — and here's what I found out.

Anna Julianna Rotolo was born May 8, 1926, or so she says. Seems the midwife spaced out and didn't record her birth for a while; so, the day, if not the year, is not certain. She was the second child, first girl, to Michele Rotolo and Paolina Bianco, both immigrants from the same town in southeastern Italy. Michele was a hod carrier and cleaned offices for a local judge; his wife took care of the kids and kept the house. My mother was subjected to old-fashioned discipline. Once she followed her older brother Pasquale across the railroad tracks and was punished by being tied with him to a chair in the basement. "It was only a few hours," she says, as she touts how she learned the important lesson of "don't get caught."

While she neither tied us up for punishment nor made us wash the floors on our hands and knees, the way the nuns made her and her siblings do when they were in the orphanage, she did raise four tough kids pretty much on her own. That, for me, was enough to turn her into a saint. However, the more I found out about her by listening to her story, the more human I realized she was, and how her failings might have contributed to the making of me. I went through some periods of anger, and then, having understood that anger, began to feel sorry for her, and came upon a new understanding of our relationship.

I learned that mothers are not cut out to be like any version or vision of perfection. No mater dolorosa, anymore; no saint, anymore. My mother is just a strong woman who has tried to make the best of whatever life has thrown at her, and I learned that by listening to her story. I went through a phase where I felt that she had been a helpless saint, then another where I felt she had used me to protect herself and her children, and, finally, I arrived at a point of acceptance of all those experiences and achieved an understanding that she had done what she could, and now I needed to do what I must.

After nearly two years, I asked my therapist the question: "When do you know when you're done with therapy?" She smiled and said, "When you start asking questions like that, you might be close." I was afraid to stop right then and there, so we cut our sessions to twice a month, then once a month, and then we stopped. I felt strong and able to go out on my own, knowing full well that help would be there if I needed it. It seemed for a while that was the case. I had developed a number of relationships with women, but nothing seemed to take me in the direction of commitment. A couple of years later, I lost the first woman I believed I had loved since my ex-wife because of my lying, so I returned to my therapist and we spent time working on issues of shame and identity.

What kept me in therapy was the realization that life requires regular maintenance; the body, soul, and mind are tools we have been given to use, and the better they work, the better life is. Therapy, for me, was a different way of maintaining my mind — something that as an intellectual I thought I could do on my own, and only those with weak minds needed help. I came to realize that I had spent forty years of my life depressed and had masked it with all the usual behaviors.

Now, I live my life—still prone to trying the intellectual solution before any others—but aware of the possibilities of getting help when I need it. Since I have learned to feel, I have been hurt and happy, depressed and jubilant; I run through the ranges of emotions like never before. I climb, I crash, but I do it all now knowing that mental illness is not a permanent state. The same way the body can become ill, undergo cure, and heal with the right help, so it is with the mind. It's this knowledge that keeps me alive, and keeps me ready to take risks that I would never have attempted before therapy.

References

Simon, Paul. 1965. "I am a Rock." The Paul Simon Songbook. London.

PART THREE

Theory and Treatment

Incorporating Culture in Mental Health Treatment of Italian Americans

KATHRYN P. ALESSANDRIA
MARIA A. KOPACZ

The U.S. population is continuously diversifying through immigration and increases in interethnic and interracial marriages. Because racial and ethnic identities are key forces shaping many individuals' values, beliefs, goals, and behaviors (Leong and Chou 1994), this growing diversity of our nation is becoming a defining issue in many areas. One of them is the field of counseling.

Professional, educational, and personal counselors provide critical services to millions of people, from students in schools and universities to accomplished adults. A central responsibility of counselors is to be aware of their own values, understand the worldviews of culturally different clients, and implement culturally appropriate intervention strategies and techniques (Sue et al. 1998). Awareness of clients' ethnic identities provides counselors with insight into the values, worldviews, and self-perceptions of clients, allowing them to implement culturally sensitive interventions.

Ample research has examined the implications of racial identities for ethnic minorities such as African Americans, Asian Americans, Latinos, and Native Americans (Hall 2001; Phinney 1990). In contrast, scholars, government officials, and practitioners have devoted little attention to ethnic identity development in white ethnic groups (Ponterotto et al. 2001). Researchers comparing ethnic groups in the United States assume that all European Americans are alike, placing them in the umbrella white category (Alessandria 2002; Alessandria and Nelson 2005). The terms white, ethnic, Caucasian, and European American are used interchangeably and are commonly associated with the characteristics of white, Anglo-Saxon Protestants (WASPs). This perception that European Americans are a homogenous group is pervasive in the counseling field, including the multicultural competency literature, where much of the research either compares other groups to whites or does not include them (Alessandria 2002, 2008).

In contrast to this categorization, the status of European Americans has been far from uniform, particularly due to the unique social and historical context of each group's immigration experiences. Upon arriving in America, many white immigrant groups, such as Italians, the Irish, and Poles, faced discrimination comparable to that faced by racial minorities in the United States. Research on intergroup communication demonstrates that when faced with such discrimination, members of a discriminated group work to reinforce and cultivate their group identity in order to protect group boundaries and group survival (Dovidio, Gaertner, and Validzic 1998). Many European immigrants have, therefore, cultivated their ethnicities, traditions, and cultures, transmitting them to their children and grandchildren, concurrently with efforts to assimilate to the majority culture (Waters and Jiménez 2005). Such diverse experiences complicate the ability to generalize about ethnic identity across white ethnic groups (Alessandria 1999; Alessandria and Nelson 2005; Phinney et al. 2001; Ponterotto et al. 2001).

If professional and educational counselors assume that European Americans are a homogenous group, many clients from this group may be receiving inappropriate counseling services because the treatment will not address the needs that emerge from their unique cultural heritage. As a result of projecting the values of the WASP group on all white ethnic clients, some clients may feel misunderstood. This could impede the process of establishing a strong therapeutic relationship, which is fundamental to creating effective counseling interventions (Hill 2004; Kokotovic and Tracey 1990). Clients who do not feel connected to their counselors are more likely to terminate counseling prematurely (Kokotovic and Tracey 1990; Sharf, Primavera, and Diener 2010), which could prolong psychological distress from unresolved issues.

Members of the college student population are still in their formative years and exploring their ethnic identities (Chickering and Reisser 1993). They may need interventions to aid with defining their emerging ethnic identities, but little literature has acknowledged the role that ethnic identities play in white ethnic students' development in college (Alessandria 2003; Ponterotto et al. 2001). The goal of this essay is to help counseling professionals orient themselves toward more culturally relevant treatment of Italian American clients, with particular emphasis on the college student population. In the sections below, we discuss the concept of ethnic identity, summarize the cultural values of Italian Americans and the evidence of their persistence in the postimmigrant population, and provide an overview of practical tools for integrating them into culturally sensitive counseling services.

DEFINING ETHNIC IDENTITY

Ethnic identity is a "dynamic multidimensional construct that refers to one's identity . . . in terms of subgroups within a larger context that claim a common ancestry and share one or more of the following elements: Culture, race, religion, language, kinship, and place of origin" (Phinney 2003, 63). A sense of self in social, historical, and cultural contexts is important to developing a healthy ego identity (Erikson 1968/ 1994). Thus, ethnic identity contributes to a person's integrated identity and self-concept, which typically develops in late adolescence/early adulthood (i.e., high school through college) (Chickering and Reisser 1993; Erikson 1968/1994; Phinney 1996, 2003). Identity development is influenced by exposure to people with different values, traditions, beliefs, and experiences (Chickering and Reisser 1993; Phinney 1996; Waters 2001). According to Phinney (2003), ethnic identity emerges as individuals become aware of ethnic groups' differences and come to appreciate the meaning or significance of their ethnicity within a greater context. Through this process, people reconsider whether to keep their own values, beliefs, and traditions or to modify them. For young adults, the interactions they have with diverse others in college play a meaningful role in decisions about whether to adjust, discard, or amplify those identities instilled by their parents (Waters 1990, 2001). Exposure to both similar and diverse peers may heighten awareness of the cultural significance of family traditions. Other factors involved in developing an ethnic identity include knowledge of the ethnic language, parental efforts to maintain cultural heritage, and social interactions with similar ethnic peers (Phinney et al. 2001). Of these three factors, peer group social interaction is the most significant, although language proficiency, which is influenced by parental cultural maintenance, is also important.

Ethnic identity is cyclical in nature; people move back and forth through three identity statuses over their life spans (Phinney 1996). Major life events such as weddings, births, and funerals are likely to initiate reflections on one's cultural values and traditions, leading to decisions about which ones to keep and transmit to future generations and which ones to let go (Safonte-Strumalo and Balaguer Dunn 2000). *Diffusion/ foreclosure* is the status when individuals have unexamined ethnic identities (Phinney 1996). Attitudes toward one's ethnicity may be neutral, positive, or negative, depending how a person's ethnicity was presented by family and community. The second stage, *moratorium*, is the status of active exploration of ethnic identity. As people come into contact with people from other backgrounds, a desire to understand the traditions, history, and current situation of their own group may begin. Finally, an individual with an *achieved ethnic identity* incorporates into his or her identity a positive view of his or her group and a commitment to a sense of belonging through participation in traditional activities and knowledge of his or her ethnic group. Acculturation attitudes (i.e., integration, assimilation, separation, or marginalization) have been related to ethnic identity and self-esteem. Research shows that an integration attitude, an attitude of embracing both the ethnic and majority cultures, has been correlated with higher self-esteem than the other attitudes (Phinney, Chavira, and Williamson 1992). Positive self-esteem is a function of a commitment and sense of belonging, more so than what the group is and how it is valued by society (Phinney, Cantu, and Kurtz 1997). Thus, it is important to help white ethnic students such as Italian Americans achieve an ethnic sense of self to contribute to healthy self-esteem. This cannot take place without understanding the values informing this group's ethnic identity.

ETHNIC IDENTITY IN ITALIAN AMERICANS

Based on Kluckhohn and Strodtbeck's (1961/1973) five-problem model of value orientations, which has been used to compare the values among a variety of white ethnic groups such as mainstream Americans, Italians, and Greeks, Italians have been characterized as follows: They tend to center upon the present time rather than the past or future (Papajohn 1999; Spiegel 1982). In contrast to mainstream Americans, they emphasize being rather than doing. Importance is placed on sharing food, working hard, enjoying life, and spending time with loved ones. The use of food by Italian Americans to express emotion and promote family togetherness is a reflection of this traditional Italian value (Alessandria 2002). In the *relational dimension*, group goals take precedence over individual goals (Papajohn 1999; Spiegel 1982). In Italian American culture, family is "an all-consuming ideal" that serves as a source of identity and security (Giordano, McGoldrick, and Guarino Klages 1996). Personal relationships with family and friends are of primary importance; only family and the few nonfamily members who are adopted into the family (e.g., godparents) are trusted. In their orientation toward *nature*, Italians see humans as unable to work against the forces of nature that overpower them (Papajohn 1999; Spiegel 1982). With regard to basic human nature, Italians believe that humans are neither innately good nor evil but have tendencies toward both. They also believe people are products of their environment. Consequently, education is considered important by postimmigrant generations of Italian Americans (Marger 2003).

Research confirms the notion of the uniqueness and persistence of Italian American cultural values. For instance, Carter and Parks' (1992) study of the persistence of cultural value preferences among postimmigrant white ethnic groups indicated that while their values weren't exactly the same as those of the immigrants or native ethnic populations, first- and later-generation Italian Americans were the most distinctly identifiable among other postimmigrant ethnic groups in the United States. Italian Americans are, therefore, a group unto themselves, not quite like native Italians and not quite like the "prototypical" WASP Americans (Papajohn 1999).

The limited research on Italian Americans indicates that Italian American ethnic identity is highly salient and valued in the Italian American population. For example, Alessandria (2003) conducted a qualitative study of the salience of ethnic identity for first-generation Italian Americans (FGIAs) and the role college plays in its development. Findings indicated that ethnic identity is salient for FGIAs. Learning Italian, interacting with Italian American peers, and their parents' efforts to instill in them a sense of their Italian culture was important in each participant's ethnic identity development. Interactions with others different from themselves contributed to developing awareness of their ethnicity. Significant events relating to participants' ethnic identity development were not limited to the college experience; rather they began in elementary school and continued through college, thus supporting the ethnic identity development factors posited by Phinney and colleagues and the literature indicating that adolescence to young adulthood is a critical period in the development of ethnic identity.

Scholars also indicate that while ethnic identity declines from the first to the second postimmigrant generation, it persists regardless of socialization to the dominant culture and adoption of its language (Alessandria 2003; Cassarino 1982; Gumina 1995; Moro 1997; Vecoli 1997). Gans (1979) suggested that second-generation Americans seek to reclaim their ethnic identity because the social costs of doing so have been mitigated. Members of the immigrant generation and their children experienced societal pressure to assimilate and be as American as possible in order to have economic and educational opportunities. The success of the first-generation Italian Americans in assimilating left the second generation with a desire to know their ethnic roots and parents who had limited information about their culture to share. However, the second and later generations are able to explore their ethnicity without social costs now that the United States embraces the "salad bowl" acculturation metaphor over the "melting pot" (McGoldrick 1993). Cassarino (1982) also argues that for second- and third-generation Italian American college students, ethnic perceptions remain integrated into their self-concept and provide a framework that is useful for interpreting oneself and one's world.

Ethnicity is a psychological dimension passed down through the generations, and maintaining a set of values characteristic of one's ethnic group may not be a conscious decision. However, several correlates have been identified for its persistence. Gumina's (1995) study of the relationships among ethnic identity, self-identity, and family values of second-generation Italian Americans aged eighteen to twenty-one in San Francisco came to the following conclusions: (1) Individuals with achieved ego identities had higher ethnic identity scores; (2) participants who perceived their parents to be highly involved in the ethnic community had higher ethnic identity scores; (3) students who were involved in the ethnic community had higher ethnic identity scores; and (4) participants who were one-hundred percent Italian had higher identity scores than those whose ancestries were mixed.

OPTIONAL ETHNICITY AND ITALIAN AMERICANS

Optional ethnicity is the concept that whites can choose to emphasize or deemphasize their ethnicity (or ethnicities) at their convenience. Waters (1990) researched optional ethnicity by interviewing sixty European American Catholics in East Coast and West Coast suburban communities and concluded that European Americans have several choices for affiliating with their ethnic group. They can choose to pass by identifying as white or American; they can choose to identify with a specific ancestry; and if multiple ancestries are present (e.g., Irish, Italian, and Polish), they can choose to identify with one or more of the identities (Waters 1990, 2001). The group(s) with which one chooses to identify can change depending on the situation and perceived desirability of affiliating with the group(s). Interestingly, when Waters (1990) asked all participants what group they would choose to belong to, if they could belong to any ethnic group, the most common response was "Italian." Another interesting finding involved individuals of mixed ancestry, where Italian was one of the groups; children in these families were most often identified as Italian, rather than mixed. This is consistent with Moro's (1997) finding that Italian Americans view themselves as Italian Americans, not white, despite the fact that they are Caucasian. This may be, in part, explained by factors such as phenotype (i.e., resemblance to the physical stereotypes of their group), surname, knowledge of family history, or societal ranking of one's ethnic group. These variables may constrain many mixed-heritage whites' ability to opt out of identifying themselves as Italian American (Alessandria 2003).

IMPLICATIONS FOR COUNSELING

A small body of evidence supports the importance of incorporating culture in counseling services provided to Italian American clients. De Meo (1998) showed that ethnic identity can be predictive of career goals in Italian Americans. Her study focused on the relationship between ethnic identity, self-esteem, and career attainment of Italian American women in New York City. An inverse relationship between traditional Italian values and career attainment existed for this sample. Women with low career attainment scores had high ethnicity scores. A positive relationship existed between career attainment and self-esteem; women with higher career attainment had higher self-esteem. Women in the youngest two age groups had the highest career attainment. Of note, no significant differences existed in the career attainment of women with single ancestry compared to that of women with mixed ancestry. This study reflects the influence of cultural values on career aspirations and the pervasiveness of cultural values in not just mental health but also career counseling. It is advised that career counselors consider client cultural values when working with Italian Americans who seek assistance in pursuing personally satisfying careers.

Ponterotto et al. (2001) conducted a study of the relationship between acculturation and attitudes toward counseling among Italian American college students. Italian American women were more likely to recognize needing professional help and were more confident that counselors could provide assistance than their male counterparts. Italian American students who were less acculturated had a higher preference for a counselor from the same ethnic background than their more acculturated peers; this was true for both males and females. Consistent with the importance placed on family in the Italian culture, Italian Americans had a preference for seeking help from peers and family members before seeking professional help. This reluctance to seek professional help should be respected and considered when establishing a therapeutic alliance with Italian American clients, particularly in the case of family or couples therapy where there may be differences among family members' perceptions of the counselor's ability to help.

Mann's (1986) experiment provides direct support for the benefits of incorporating ethnic elements into counseling among Italian Americans. The author tested the use of ethnotherapy groups with first- and second-generation Italian Americans to improve self-esteem, ethnic identity, and sense of control in this population. The results indicated that the ethnotherapy participants had significant increases in self-esteem and ethnic identity compared to the control condition. The implication of this research is that mental health professionals need to incorporate clients' ethnicities in the services they provide to individuals of Italian descent beyond the immigrant generation by acknowledging the influence ethnicity may have on individuals' self-concept (Cassarino 1982; Papajohn 1999). This may be of particular importance with adolescent and young adult populations who, developmentally, are in a highly active period of defining their identities.

TOOLS FOR INCORPORATING CULTURE IN TREATMENT

Taken together, the literature on ethnic identity in Italian Americans suggests that it is a persistent construct that develops through a cyclical process and that influences a host of personal and professional outcomes for individuals. It is, therefore, important to consider specific recommendations for culturally aware counseling of Italian American clients.

Scholarship on multicultural counseling competence lists the following indicators of counselor cultural competence: (1) An ability to anticipate client issues without making assumptions; (2) an ability to apply cultural characteristics to a client while acknowledging the client's individual traits; and (3) knowledge of the historical, social, and political issues affecting the client. These skills are necessary to be effective with the cultural groups with which one is working (Arredondo et al. 1996; Hays 2001; Holcomb-McCoy 2000). As a practical extension of these competencies, Hardy and Laszloffy (1995) developed a cultural genogram that can be used to acquire information for counseling interventions. Several of their recommendations are outlined here. However, it is recommended that the reader go to the original source for further details.

When working with families, couples, and individuals, genograms have been used to understand clients, gather information, enhance joining, and evaluate client issues. The goal of the cultural genogram is to exemplify and clarify the influence of culture on the family system (Hardy and Laszloffy 1995). This genogram can be used to collect information about clients' cultural backgrounds and conceptualize client issues. It can also be used as a tool to promote self-awareness among counselors by creating their own. The uniqueness of the cultural genogram is that it emphasizes acknowledging all the cultures in a client's background. Intercultural relationships are identified on the genogram, as are each family member's cultural background, by using client-selected symbols and colors. The genogram's author develops a cultural framework chart, similar to a map legend, to the genogram and all its symbols. Discussing the client's organizing principles and pride/shame issues can shed light on the values associated with the cultures represented in the genogram (Hardy and Laszloffy 1995). For example, does the client identify more with one culture over another represented in the genogram? If so, to what does the client attribute this? A selection of the questions from Hardy and Laszloffy (1995, 232) to consider when creating a cultural genogram include:

- . . . [U]nder what conditions did your family (or their descendants) enter the US (immigrant, political refugee, slave, etc.)? For example, did the family immigrate in the last wave of Italians (mid 1960s to 1970s) or were they Italians who came in the late nineteenth/early twentieth century? Did they have a support network in the US? What are the expected gender roles in the culture, and did the family adhere to them? As the generations become farther from the immigrant experience, it may be important to consider whether they live in an ethnic community and if they have had interactions with same-ethnic peers.

• What were/are the group's experiences with oppression or discrimination due to their ethnic status?

• What role does religion and spirituality play in the everyday lives of members of the group?

• What prejudices or stereotypes does this group have about itself? About other groups? What stereotypes/prejudices do others have about this group? The recentness of the immigration event may influence perceptions about discrimination experienced and the stories that have been passed down through the generations about these experiences.

• What role (if any) do names play in the group? Are there rules, mores, or rituals about assigning names?

• How do members of this group view outsiders in general and mental health providers specifically?

• How much emphasis was placed on maintaining ethnic traditions and values?

In tandem with the cultural genogram, it is advised to create a timeline of significant events in the client's life related to culture and the immigration process. The counselor should find out: Who immigrated and when, why they immigrated to the United States, and where they came from and where they settled. For example, did they settle in San Francisco or the Northeast? Did they live in ethnic neighborhoods or areas where there were few other Italians? Was there an extended family network in the area? Through this, one can not only understand the timeline and hardships experienced but can also place the events in the social and historical context of both the United States and the country of origin. Further, it is advisable to find out what life has been like for their cultural group in this country, as well as what life has been like for this particular individual/family.

A third effective tool for incorporating culture into counseling is Hays' (2001) ADDRESSING (Age and generational influences, Developmental and acquired Disabilities, Religion and spiritual orientation,

Ethnicity, Socioeconomic status, Sexual orientation, Indigenous heritage, National origin, and Gender) framework. This framework is useful for gathering information that promotes understanding of clients in their particular social and historical context. Understanding clients' multiple identities along the ADDRESSING framework provides the counselor with a deeper understanding of the cultural influences on clients' lives, worldviews, and presenting concerns. Awareness of these characteristics promotes culturally conscious case conceptualization. Another consideration is that the salience of clients' multiple identities may differ based on setting and environmental expectations. When applying this framework to clients, counselors should consider the following [see Hays (2001, 60)]:

1. What are the ADDRESSING influences on this client?

2. What are this client's salient identities related to each of these influences? What are the possible meanings of these identities in the dominant culture, in the client's culture, and from the personal perspective of the client? For example, a second-generation Italian American female who is deaf could identify more with being deaf and female than her ethnic status.

3. How are my salient identities interacting with those of the client?

a. How am I being perceived by this client, based on my visible identity? For example, a first-generation Italian American female counselor whose married name is Irish, may wish to share information about her Italian ethnic identity with her Italian American clients, given Ponterotto et al.'s (2001) findings on the preference of Italian American clients for same-ethnic counselors.

b. Am I knowledgeable about those groups with which the client identifies?

c. How might my identity and related experiences, values, and beliefs limit my understanding of this client?

Counselors should also ask clients about their generation of immigration and contact with their country and culture of origin, which can illuminate the influences of ethnicity, national origin, and generational influences on the client. Consider, for example, a second-generation Italian American college student who was raised in an ethnic neighborhood in an urban area by immigrant grandparents while his or her parents worked full time in a family business. She or he is the first person to attend college in the family. This client may have a very different worldview and college experience than a third-generation Italian/Irish American who never met his or her immigrant great-grandparents, whose parents both graduated from college, and who was raised in a suburban community.

When working with couples or families, intracultural conflicts may arise from differences in family-of-origin immigration patterns and the influences of these immigration experiences on clients' perceptions of their ethnic group's values (Softas-Nall and Baldo 2000). For example, an Italian American couple, where one partner is an Italian immigrant who was raised in modern-day Italy and the other is a third-generation Italian American whose family immigrated in the early 1900s, may have very different perceptions of their culture based on their respective experiences with the country of origin (or lack thereof) and the values passed down from family members.

With clients whose culture places as strong an emphasis on family as the Italian culture does, it may be important to involve other members of the family in the treatment process. Safonte-Strumalo and Dunn (2000) provided a case study of an Italian American family grieving the unanticipated loss of a child. The parents were first-generation Italian Americans who identified strongly with their Italian heritage and presented for counseling with their other children. The therapist was a third-generation Italian American woman. Through constructing a genogram with the family, they discussed the emotional impact of the loss, which they had never done before; the significance of the Italian culture to this family surfaced. All grandparents were from Italy, and approximately ninety-five percent of the family was Italian. Using a systems approach, the therapist explored culture and gender as they pertained to how loss was dealt with in this family. Intergenerational issues were explored based on the physical proximity and importance of extended family relationships to the nuclear family. Safonte-Strumalo and Dunn (2000) described the therapist's interventions to address bereavement with both the nuclear and extended family:

> By taking into consideration relational and cultural issues in the family's coping with loss, the therapist and family were able to learn about important relational, gender, and cultural influences

that affected their grieving process. Family members gained insight into the strength of these patterns, and the therapist was able to design interventions that were congruent with the relational and cultural values of the family. (338–339)

Counselors should attend to intergenerational differences in values, reactions, and observance of cultural traditions related to death and loss when working with families.

To effectively evaluate client issues, Hays (2001) advocates seeking information from a variety of sources, including school, parents and significant family members, health-care providers, behavioral observations, client's age and development in relation to historical events, and medical and psychological information. In addition to helping counselors gain self-awareness, the ADDRESSING framework emphasizes awareness of privileges related to one's multiple identities. Counselors should engage in learning about clients' cultural histories outside of sessions; sociological and historical sources can be used to gain information about the social, cultural, and political influences on clients. Finally, it is not enough to just be aware of the ADDRESSING influences on clients' lives; it is important to look for culturally related strengths and support systems for clients.

No matter what issues a client brings to counseling, the most important thing is to build a strong therapeutic relationship and to earn the client's trust. This is achieved by being genuine, empathetic, showing unconditional positive regard and respect, and by creating a warm atmosphere in which clients can feel comfortable expressing their vulnerabilities. Being open to exploring the role of culture in client issues by being willing to engage in a dialogue about it and listening for cues from the client that indicate their values and worldview, so as to be able to implement culturally appropriate interventions, is of the utmost importance. Finally, a word of caution. Incorporating culture in counseling is a delicate balance between listening to the significance clients place on their culture, understanding the social and historical experiences of the group, and looking for the unique experiences that brought the client to the counselor's office (Alessandria 2008).

References

Alessandria, Kathryn P. 1999. "Identity Development and Self-Esteem of First-Generation American College Students: A Comparison with non First-Generation Students." Ed.S. Thesis. James Madison University.

_____. 2002. "Acknowledging White Ethnic Groups in Multicultural Counseling." *The Family Journal* 10:57–60.

_____. 2003. "Ethnic Identity Salience for Italian Americans: A Qualitative Analysis." Ph.D. Dissertation. University of Virginia.

_____. 2008. "White Ethnic Groups." In *The Encyclopedia of Social Work,* Vol. 4., edited by Terry Mizrahi and Larry. E. Davis, 279–281. Washington, DC: NASW Press; New York: Oxford University Press.

_____, and E. S. Nelson. 2005. "Identity Development and Self-Esteem of First-Generation American College Students: An Exploratory Study." *Journal of College Student Development* 461:3–12.

Arredondo, Patricia, Rebecca Toporek, Sherlon P. Brown, Janet Sanchez, Don C. Locke, Joe Sanchez, and Holly Stadler. 1996. "Operationalization of the Multicultural Counseling Competencies." *Journal of Multicultural Counseling and Development* 24:42–78.

Carter, Robert T., and Elizabeth E. Parks. 1992. "White Ethnic Group Membership and Cultural Value Preferences." *Journal of College Student Development* 33:499–506.

Cassarino, Paul R. 1982. "The Relationship Between Ethnicity and Self-Concept in Italian-Americans." Ph.D. Dissertation. University of Rhode Island.

Chickering, Arthur W., and Linda Reisser. 1993. *Education and Identity,* 2nd ed. San Francisco: Jossey-Bass.

De Meo, Carol. 1998. "The Relationship of Ethnic Identity, Self-Esteem and Career Attainment Among Italian-American Women." Ph.D. Dissertation. New York University.

Dovidio, John F., Samuel L. Gaertner, and Ana Validzic. 1998. "Intergroup Bias: Status, Differentiation, and a Common In-Group Identity." *Journal of Personality and Social Psychology* 75:109–120.

Erikson, Erik H. 1968/1994. *Identity: Youth and Crisis.* New York: W. W. Norton.

Gans, Herbert J. 1979. "Symbolic Ethnicity: The Future of Ethnic Groups and Cultures in America." In *On the Making of Americans: Essays in Honor of David Riesman,* edited by Herbert. J. Gans, Nathan Glazer, Joseph. R. Gusfield, and Christopher Jencks, 193–220. Philadelphia: University of Pennsylvania Press.

Giordano, Joe, Monica McGoldrick, and Joanne Guarino Klages. 1996. "Italian Families." In *Ethnicity and Family Therapy,* 2nd ed., edited by Monica McGoldrick, Joe Giordano, and John K. Pearce, 567–582. New York: Guilford.

Gumina, Deanna P. 1995. "Ethnic Identity, Self-Identity, and Family Values: A Study of Italian-American Late Adolescents in the San Francisco Bay Area." Ph.D. Dissertation. California School for Professional Psychology.

Hall, Gordon C. N. 2001. "Psychotherapy Research with Ethnic Minorities: Empirical, Ethical, and Conceptual Issues." *Journal of Consulting and Clinical Psychology* 69:502–510.

Hardy, Kenneth V., and Tracey A. Laszloffy. 1995. "The Cultural Genogram: Key to Training Culturally Competent Family Therapists." *Journal of Marital and Family Therapy* 21:227–237.

Hays, Pamela A. 2001. *Addressing Cultural Complexities in Practice: A framework for clinicians and counselors.* Washington, DC: American Psychological Association.

Hill, Clara E. 2004. *Helping Skills: Facilitating Exploration, Insight, and Action,* 2nd ed. Washington, DC: American Psychological Association.

Holcomb-McCoy, Cheryl C. 2000. "Multicultural Counseling Competencies: An Exploratory Factor Analysis." *Journal of Multicultural Counseling and Development* 28:83–97.

Kluckhohn, Florence R., and Fred L. Strodtbeck. 1961/1973. *Variations in Value Orientations.* Westport, CT: Greenwood Press.

Kokotovic, Anna M., and Terence J. Tracey. 1990. "Working Alliance in the Early Phase of Counseling." *Journal of Counseling Psychology* 371:16–21.

Leong, Frederick T. L., and Elayne L. Chou. 1994. "The Role of Ethnic Identity and Acculturation in the Vocational Behavior of Asian Americans: An Integrative Review." *Journal of Vocational Behavior* 44:155–172.

Mann, Lisa. 1986. "Ethnotherapy with Italian-Americans: An Evaluation of Short-Term Group Exploration of Ethnic Identification and Self-Esteem." Ph.D Dissertation. New York University.

Marger, Martin N. 2003. "Italian Americans." In *Race and Ethnic Relations: American and Global Perspectives* 6th ed. Belmont, CA: Wadsworth. 2003. 201-226.

McGoldrick, Monica. 1993. "Ethnicity, Cultural Diversity, and Normality", in *Normal Family Processes,* 2nd ed., edited by Froma Walsh, 331-360. New York: Guilford Press.

Moro, Margaret V. 1997. "The Italian-American Family over Three Generations: Family Competence, Individuation, Ethnic Identity and Self-esteem." Ph.D Dissertation. Seton Hall University.

Papajohn, John C. 1999. *The Hyphenated American: The Hidden Injuries of Culture.* Westport, CT: Greenwood Press.

Phinney, Jean S. 1990. "Ethnic Identity in Adolescents and Adults: Review of Research." *Psychological Bulletin* 108:499–514.

_____, Victor Chavira, and Lisa Williamson. 1992. "Acculturation attitudes and self-esteem among high school and college students." *Youth & Society* 23: 299-312.

_____. 1996. "Understanding Ethnic Diversity: The Role of Ethnic Identity." *American Behavioral Scientist* 40:143–152.

_____. 2003. "Ethnic Identity and Acculturation." In *Acculturation: Advances in Theory, Measurement, and Applied Research,* edited by Kevin Chun, Pamela Ball, and Gerardo Marin, 63–81. Washington, DC: American Psychological Association.

_____, Cindy L. Cantu, and Dawn A. Kurtz. 1997. "Ethnic and American Identity as Predictors of Self-Esteem Among African American, Latino, and White Adolescents." *Journal of Youth and Adolescence* 26:165–185.

_____, Irma Romero, Monica Nava, and Dan Huang. 2001. "The Role of Language, Parents, and Peers in Ethnic Identity Among Adolescents in Immigrant Families." *Journal of Youth and Adolescence* 30:135–153.

Ponterotto, Joseph G., Vincent Rao, Julie Zweig, Brian P. Rieger, Kristin Schaefer, Sophie Michelakou, Carolyn Armenia, and Harold Goldstein. 2001. "The Relationship of Acculturation and Gender to Attitudes toward Counseling in Italian and Greek American College Students." *Cultural Diversity and Ethnic Minority Psychology* 7:362–375.

Safonte-Strumolo, Nicole, and Adrianna Balaguer Dunn. 2000. "Consideration of Cultural and Relational Issues in Bereavement: The Case of an Italian American Family." *The Family Journal: Counseling and Therapy for Couples and Families* 8:334–340.

Sharf, Jennie, Louis H. Primavera, and Marc J. Diener. 2010. "Dropout and Therapeutic Alliance: A Meta-Analysis of Adult Individual Psychotherapy." *Psychotherapy, Theory, Research, Practice, Training* 474:637–645.

Spiegel, John. 1982. "An Ecological Model of Ethnic Families." In *Ethnicity and Family Therapy,* edited by Monica McGoldrick, John K. Pearce, and Joseph Giordano, 31–51. New York: Guilford Press.

Softas-Nall, Basilia C., and Tracy D. Baldo. 2000. "Dialogues within a Greek Family: Multicultural Stories of a Couple Revisited." *The Family Journal: Counseling and Therapy for Couples and Families* 8:396–398.

Sue, Derald W., Robert T. Carter, J. Manuel Casas, Nadya A. Fouad, Allen E. Ivey, Margaret Jensen, Teresa LaFromboise, Jeanne E. Manese, Joseph G. Ponterotto, Ena Vasquez-Nutall. 1998. "Ethnocentric Monoculturalism." In *Multicultural Aspects of Counseling Series: Vol. 11. Multicultural Counseling Competencies: Individual and Organizational Development,* edited by Paul Pederson, 14–25. Thousand Oaks, CA: Sage.

Vecoli, Rudolph J. 1997. "Are Italian Americans Just White Folks?" In *Beyond the Godfather: Italian American Writers on the Real Italian American Experience,* edited by A. Kenneth Ciongoli and Jay Parini, 307–318. Hanover, NH: University Press of New England.

Waters, Mary C. 1990. *Ethnic Options: Choosing Identities in America.* Berkeley, CA: University of California Press.

_____. 2001. "Optional Ethnicities: For Whites Only?" In *Race Class and Gender: An Anthology,* edited by Margaret L. Andersen and Patricia H. Collins, 430–439. Belmont, CA: Wadsworth/Thompson Learning.

_____, and Tomás R. Jiménez 2005. "Assessing Immigrant Assimilation: New Empirical and Theoretical Challenges." *Annual Review of Sociology* 31:105–125.

Italians Tend to Keep Their Dead with Them: Navigating Grief and Loss in Italian American Culture

DONNA DICELLO
LORRAINE MANGIONE

> You found me in bed
> with full sleep over me
> at about 4 a.m.,
> New York time.
> Without even knocking,
> you entered my head.
> You were fresh and content
> as I have rarely seen you.
> . . .
> You put your head on my pillow
> as if you were going to reveal the mystery of life
> to me . . .
> — "The Visit"

In this poem by Marisa Frasca (2008, 25), we are witness to a night-time visit by the poet's mother in which they go on to talk, dance, laugh, and carry on as if they were still together in life; the emotional tone is one of warmth and normalcy. An example of how "Italians tend to keep their dead with them" (Giordano, McGoldrick, and Guarino Klages 2005, 623) — they visit in dreams and then are written about in poetry — this poem frames the Italian American experience regarding death that we believe has much to offer to Western conceptualizations of death and grieving.

Most ethnic and/or religious cultures have their characteristic ways of facing death and its aftermath, and Italians are no different in having their own traditions around this universal experience. For the present authors, images of the deaths from our childhoods, including our grandmothers, grandfathers, great aunts and uncles, and old family friends, who were like great aunts and uncles, came pouring over us as we read and reflected on the title for this essay. It seemed to indicate something huge and compelling from our upbringing as Italian Americans in the second half of the twentieth century, and perhaps something more particular to the Italian culture than to others: Death is important, a monumental event in the lives of most people; but for those of us who are Italian, continuing to love those who have died and keeping up the connection is just as important and vital for our survival. We remember in-home altars to family and to those who were gone, with candles and pictures, and sometimes flowers, that lasted forever. We remember speaking *about* those who had died as if they were still alive and also speaking *to* those who had died. Heaven seemed not so far away and fairly accessible to all of us; closer certainly and with more contact than the world of Italy they left behind had seemed to those who made the passage in steerage. We thought of two aunts who spoke of their mother every single day for decades after she died, until one of them also died, and that kept them all connected and kept their mother alive and active in their lives. We reflected on an older cousin who had collected a world of art objects after the loss of her husband, and what that work and creativity meant to her. We considered another aunt, in her nineties, who "speaks" daily to her husband in their large, framed, painted wedding photograph; a husband gone almost forty years. Now, with the passing of our own aunts, uncles, and parents, we see how deeply we want to hold on to them, to keep them alive, to not let them disappear into the vast vat of past and memory. We want them alive and well and vibrant, if only in our hearts and minds.

For both of us, our trajectories of grieving for our fathers have brought this idea of keeping the dead with us very much to the forefront. We both had strong, positive, consequential relationships with our fathers, and we both lost our fathers in the last ten years. These relationships encompassed a multitude of feelings and experiences, including conflicts, arguments, and disagreements, along with the warmth and caring; they were full and full-bodied father–daughter relationships. Our grief has been similar, filled with a whole spectrum of feelings, thoughts, memories, and images, including both regrets and gratefulness; at times borne in private but also shared with others who knew and loved our fathers.

Sometimes when one is brought up in a home or in a culture that is not typical of mainstream America, one does not realize it until years later. We were brought up in such homes and such a culture. When it comes to death, many Italian Americans do not subscribe to the get over it or find closure approach, and neither did we, but both of us came to realize that many friends, colleagues, and acquaintances in our contemporary world did subscribe to such an approach, and we were a little outside of the norm of the larger culture. There can be a tendency to pathologize anything that does not seem efficient and tidy within grief and mourning in our current culture or anything that does not follow prescribed stages (Konigsberg 2011). The quotation from Giordano et al. (2005), cited earlier, helped us to normalize and depathologize grief and loss as Italian Americans and alerted us to the fact that others might have similar situations to ours—caught between the Italian American world of relatedness and connection and the mainstream American world of endings as final and finished.

While there is some literature that examines cross-cultural experiences of grief (Rosenblatt 2008), Italian American conceptualizations of grief have not been examined in any systematic way in the psychological literature. As Italian American women, we began to write about our experiences with grieving for our fathers, viewing it as a potential model for what Italian culture has to contribute to American views on grief and mourning. In addition, we considered it to be a potential teaching tool for helping others in their grief, whatever their ethnic backgrounds. In doing so, we discovered the key role that actively transmuting our grief into something concrete has played in processing our grief. In our grieving, in our attempt to hold our fathers near to us, each of us has developed a project or a practice that incorporates our father and our relationship to him. For one of us, it has been cooking: Immersion in the whole experience of cooking great foods like her dad did, using his recipes, as well as others, feeding people, and loving the atmosphere and community that gathers around food. For the other, it has been the writing of koans (short sayings meant to challenge one's perspective and thinking, leading to spiritual enhancement)—the act of sitting and contemplating and writing, sometimes when immersed in grief, but at other times simply because it was the right time to write. Each of these activities has kept our fathers with us as we have navigated our profound sense of loss and sorrow at their deaths. Each of these activities and acts of remembrance has helped our fathers stay alive in our hearts—at our desks and in our kitchen, as we have written, cooked, and otherwise spent time involved in these acts. The activities have held us and nurtured us through very dark times.

In this essay, we present our ideas about grieving in the Italian American culture and, particularly, focus on how the doing of a significant creative project or activity can be a welcome partner on the long path of grief and reconnection to the person who has died. We do this first through questions that we pose about the Italian American experience of death, through which we provide some concepts about Italians and their relationship to death, and then offer ideas about metaphors that are central to our view of working with grief and keeping the dead near. Narratives regarding the metaphors we used to grieve our fathers are included, as well as proposed clinical suggestions for working with clients who are Italian American and dealing with the death of a loved one.

Finally, a case example of an Italian American woman who sought psychotherapy from one of the authors is also discussed.

QUESTIONS ABOUT DEATH, GRIEVING,
AND THE ITALIAN AMERICAN CULTURE

Certain questions guide our discussion of Italian Americans, death, and grieving and provide a framework for the ideas that have begun to be articulated in the introduction. The first has to do with understanding death and grief better in the Italian and Italian American cultures, how it is expressed, and why it seems to have the place that it does. The second explores whether there are parts of Italian American culture that promote what feels like a real sense of resiliency with regard to grief. The final one looks at whether and how Italian American ways of grief and mourning can have an impact on the more dominant culture's customs and practices. Our intent is to intertwine thoughts about these questions into the final section, after musing about them a bit more here.

Why is grief such a central aspect of the Italian and Italian American cultures? We think about history, family, religion, mysticism, myth, and destiny in conjunction with this question. As Italy celebrated the 150th anniversary of unification, it was a reminder that the last few centuries of Italian history have included the battles among different groups of Italians and then the military campaign to unite Italians (Mangione and Morreale 1992). It is often noted that Italians, particularly southern Italians, have relied tremendously on family as their primary social unit, given the external strife and mistrust around them (Gambino 1997). Part of that family life has been an emphasis on religion and spirituality, whether through Catholicism and its more mystic, ritualistic aspects or through folk wisdom. Certainly in Catholicism, death and rebirth are at the center. As people who believe in the power of destiny or fate, death may be an inevitable outcome over which one has no control. Another part of family life has to do with the intensity of the relationships within the family, and death is, possibly, the ultimate act of separation, and therefore something to which one must attend (Giordano et al. 2005).

Are there certain aspects of Italian American culture that foster resiliency as it pertains to grief? Just as an emphasis on family and close relationships may make one more attuned to death, it may also be what allows one to survive the death of one's most cherished family and friends and carry on with life. A sense of mysticism and spirituality, such as the hope that the departed person resides in a better world, or has gone to see God face to face, or is reuniting with old family or friends can also make for a capacity to accept death and its consequences. There is a mystery to this life and the next, and we don't have all the answers rationally laid out for us, and it seems that many Italians embrace this perspective.

Do Italian American conceptualizations of mourning have something to offer to current Western perspectives on grief? Italian American writers have addressed the issue of whether or not to view Italian Americans as part of the dominant white culture in America or as a group distinct from that, as well as how important a role ethnicity plays in the lives and identities of Italian Americans (Alba 2000; Bayor 2009; Barreca 2002; Boscia-Mulé 1999; Gambino 1997; Guglielmo 2003; Luconi 2004; Vecoli 2000). From this viewpoint of mourning and grief, Italian Americans do not necessarily align with the dominant cultural ethos, which might be described as progression through linear stages to the point of closure. Bona (2010) illustrates this when she describes Italian American deaths in literature, with literary characters often exhibiting a varied and complex path of mourning. With overly scheduled and busy lives, less and less time and energy is devoted to mourning and grief in contemporary American culture; thus, this perspective may indeed inform how grief and mourning have come to be viewed and experienced in the dominant culture. As a counterpoint to the dominant culture, Bona (2010) further purports that, "like Persephone returning, writers of Italian America portray death as a story of continuity, a story about how things change, but don't end" (208).

STAPLES OF ITALIAN AMERICAN CULTURE
AND THE CAPACITY FOR SYMBOLIZATION

Three aspects of Italian American culture discussed above—family as central to life and to survival, resilience tempered with fate as a framework for living, and the power and transformability of metaphor and symbol—underlie our thinking about Italians tending to keep their dead near them.

FAMILY AS CENTRAL. While this has almost become a cliché, it is rooted deeply in the Italian American psyche. Family, which includes extended family and even close friends, who tend to become part of the family, is considered one's greatest resource in life and critical to survival in an often harsh world (Giordano et al. 2005; Gambino 1997; Alba 2000). The deep level of connectedness is at the center of one's psyche and one's life.

RESILIENCE AND FATE. Resilience is the capacity to come back after defeat, to pick up the pieces and try again, to see the glass half full, to practice optimism despite setbacks, all of which easily describes the Italian American population that has worked so hard and achieved so much in the last century or so. Giordano et al. (2005) noted that "adaptability and stoicism became ethnic trademarks" (342) for Italian Americans. Early immigrant work ethic, the capacity for labor organizing, and the creation of mutual aid societies show the ability to adapt and compete in a strange new world (Mangione and Morreale 1992).

Fate or destiny is perhaps the larger frame within which resilience resides, and both fate and resilience come into play in grief and mourning. There is a sense that grief is integrated into life and that loss is a part of living. Death and the ensuing sorrow are natural, unavoidable events—they are part of our fate, and we all experience them and survive somehow.

DRAMA, SYMBOL, AND MEANING MAKING. In a culture imbued with rich visual arts and architecture, a mysterious and ritual-laden religion, hand and facial gestures that defy outsider understanding, ancient beliefs in oracles and soothsayers, and stories of gods and goddesses who once roamed the earth, it is easy to see the centrality of symbolization and the intricacies of meaning making. Early southern immigrants' religion has been described as being "based on awe, fear, and reverence for the supernatural, 'a fusion of Christian and pre-Christian elements of animism, polytheism, and sorcery along with the sacraments prescribed by the Church'" (Mangione and Morreale 1992, 326). Perhaps because there was so much in life that was inscrutable and mysterious, Italians seem to have developed the practice of drama, symbol, and ritual as important vehicles for life events and the central part of their religion, particularly regarding death (Giordano et al. 2005). Things do not always mean what they first seem to mean or what they mean on the surface. The use of metaphor as a vehicle for meaning making can resonate in a culture in which the unconscious, the unknown, the unknowable, and the inscrutable are freely at play.

METAPHOR AND ITS MEANING IN GRIEF

The concept of metaphor is not new to the psychological literature (Berlin et al. 1991; Siegelman 1993). The use of metaphor in psychotherapy transcends orientation and in fact has been touted as a way to more completely understand client material, to overcome impasses, and to deepen the therapeutic experience. As discussed in the literature, the fundamental nature of metaphor is to bring new understanding to an issue or idea that remains elusive or not well understood. Siegelman (1993) states that "by its very nature, metaphor combines what is already known in a new way to produce a new thing not yet fully understood" (67). According to Lakoff and Johnson (1980), "the essence of metaphor is understanding one kind of thing or experience in terms of another" (5). In this respect, metaphor becomes a means of communication by importing meanings from a primary domain to a new domain (Berlin et al. 1991; Rosenblatt 2008) and emphasizes the relationships between situations rather than emphasizing only a discrete set of facts (Berlin et al. 1991). As they apply to psychotherapy, metaphors become more than simply figures of speech or creative ways to make interpretations; they are structural devices for the therapist to help the client make meaning of their experience and to use as a guide in the therapy.

The use and application of metaphor has also been integrated into the grief therapy literature, with metaphor being viewed as a medium that interfaces language, affect, and perceived experience. It is not uncommon for the bereaved who seek psychotherapy (or who experience a loss during the course of treatment) to speak metaphorically of their loss or their loved one. Nadeau (2006) contends that therapists can use these metaphors to aid clients in making meaning of their loss and of their experiences with the grieving process. In addition, metaphors may allow for a new understanding of grief as a difficult process and allow healing in a more comprehensive way. Since a client's affect and experience may not always be consciously known, metaphors may serve as guideposts for the therapist to what cannot be directly expressed. By listening for metaphors, therapists may hear unconscious meanings that might otherwise have been obscured by a focus on content (Nadeau 2006). In listening for and considering the metaphors that an individual may use in therapy, the therapist may be able to understand how grief is viewed, how the client conceptualizes his or her grief, and how it might transmute and change over time. Nadeau (2006) also states that ". . . they [metaphors] provide a potentially less threatening way of talking about the loss experience, and they can be used to suggest alternative ways of responding to the loss" (205).

While metaphors can certainly contribute to positive progress as a client processes his or her grief, Nadeau (2006) also contends that there are possible risks in the use of metaphor. It is critical for the therapist to monitor whether or not a metaphor has been misinterpreted and assess as to whether or not the interpretation may be meaningful to the client. In that regard, Nadeau (2006) recommends the need to develop a trained ear, one that can allow the client to lead the direction the metaphor and its applicability may need to take.

The use of metaphor became central to us as we each processed the grief in our fathers' deaths. For one of us (Lorraine), cooking is an immersive experience, living in and with the eggplant and basil and olive oil, living with her dad and his love for food and eating and for feeding others. For the other (Donna), the Buddhist practice of koans served as a vehicle for understanding the enormity of such a loss and anchored her in the present, allowing her to bear her grief one breath at a time. We take the idea of metaphor further to speak of "extended metaphor," a concept from literature that involves a metaphor that extends over time, such as a poem that elaborates on a metaphor throughout the poem (Stanford Artificial Intelligence Laboratory 2011). We conceptualize it as a metaphor with multiple levels that is processed and transmuted over time in one's life and one's psyche. Our stories of our own grieving for our fathers are briefly included here to offer a flavor of what is meant by grieving through the use of metaphor. Although we are talking about cooking and koans, the metaphor could be anything that resonates with the grieving person and connects him or her up to his or her own feelings as well as to the person who is gone.

LORRAINE'S STORY: RED CLAM SAUCE AND MY FATHER

The night my father died, ten years ago, we had all just finished eating a marvelous dinner of spaghettini with red clam sauce that we had made according to his specifications. The week before he died, he had recuperated enough from several months of illness and debilitation after a surgery that he was able to prepare and serve his homemade baked stuffed clams at my brother's wedding party of over a hundred people. The last year of his life, during a time when he wasn't physically able to cook, he talked us through such dishes as pork pizzaioloa, broccoli arape[1] and ceci, and all sorts of things with eggplant. For his second career, starting from age fifty, he was the owner/cook (he hated the word *chef*) of a Sicilian restaurant in a town in Connecticut that hadn't seen anything like his food before (it was like bringing a bit of the real Little Italy on the Lower East Side, where he grew up, to the suburbs); and for all of his adult life he did the special cooking in our house. Several years ago, he roasted a whole goat in our oven, which was scary because it resembled our family dog; but was it ever tasty! When my sister married forty years ago, he had his food in just about every refrigerator and freezer in our neighborhood for the party at the house after the reception.

So in some ways, it wasn't all that surprising that after his death I found myself doing such things as: Suddenly crying in the supermarket or the farmer's markets, unable to choose and sometimes needing to leave the store; weeping as I sliced tomatoes, especially the real summer tomatoes that Italians live for; getting obsessed with perfect timing for cooking pasta; making phone calls to family members and close friends for any of his recipes that they may have gotten over the years, while searching frantically for those that were lost, or, feeling the frustration when we knew the ingredients but not the process very well, such as in making homemade ricotta; jotting down everything my brothers and sister, or anyone else, could remember about things he said and did that had to do with food; and definitely cooking his food as often as possible. It helped that my daughter decided that pasta with peas and onions, a very simple peasant dish, was her top choice for dinner almost any night. Five years after his death, our family and friends even hosted a large memorial birthday dinner for my dad, for which the guests all cooked and contrib-

---

[1] *Rapini* or *broccoli di rape*. My dad spelled it this way on his restaurant menu as it was unusual on menus for central Connecticut in the 1970's, and he wanted it spelled the way he pronounced it, thus the "arape."

uted one of their favorite dishes from his recipes. It was as if he had joined us for the night.

Somewhere along the way it occurred to me that cooking was part of my way of grieving for my father. Even though I certainly hadn't started out thinking, oh, cooking, what a great way to mourn my dad, it really became that. It was a process that allowed me to connect with him, be with him, be in conversation with others about my dad, and experience a whole range of emotions that swirled about him. I could hear his voice congratulating me on rolled, stuffed eggplant well done and chiding me as a bit lazy when I chopped rather than minced the garlic. I could argue with him, as we used to do in life, about a great spectrum of things, such as politics and history, friends and family, and philosophy and meaning of life, as I stirred sauce or considered how much rosemary to use on a pork roast. Cooking had become my path of grieving—of mourning his loss, but keeping him close. It gave me something to do while my heart was broken and needed time and space to heal. My father was so much more than food and feeding—he loved history and art, and he thrived on debating politics, ethics, values, and morals. He was a disciplinarian and could be a tough guy, but it was the food and feeding people that I drank in through my pores, internalized as a child and a teenager, and it was food and memories of him cooking and serving that made me weep, yet also emerged to hold me in my sorrow.

DONNA'S STORY: THE LONG AND WINDING ROAD OR
WHAT IS THE SOUND OF ONE HEART BREAKING?

Death is mysterious—it has a way of paradoxically making time stand still and also pass at the speed of light. Immediately following the death of my father, time had that quality to me, resulting in my days feeling surreal and shrouded. If only I part the veil, I thought, this will have been a bad dream. Hours would pass, and I would think that it had only been one. Or conversely, when the pain felt the greatest, I would watch the clock, certain that it had not moved one second, and that the batteries must be running low; but that was not the case, of course. Sitting in my office at work, I would look at the phone and think, "My father is not going to call me today." I tried hard to remember the last time he had left me a voicemail, and I agonized over the fact that I had not saved it. I would never hear my father's voice again; never. It felt, at times, that my sanity could be compromised with that thought. Gone was his belly laugh, his opinionated view of things, his attempts to remember the Italian he had spoken long ago with his mother. In my mind, I would strain to hear his voice, but after his death it so quickly became ephemeral, like a vapor rising from the grass in the early morning—rising, rising—until it becomes one with the air, none of its remnants remaining in the midday sun.

When my father died, my mother became a widow after fifty-one years of marriage. My parents came as a matched set—always together, finishing each other's sentences, a sense between them that they really liked each other. It certainly was not a perfect relationship, but together they had formed the warp and weft of a life that worked for them. My mother took my father's death hard, often telling me that she still thought she heard him talking to her in bed at night, and we would laugh over cups of tea that even in death he probably still had a lot to say. I knew that it was not the voice of psychosis that was speaking to her, but the primal emptiness that comes from losing someone who was in your pores, who was your other half, with whom you could not imagine a life without.

When her birthday came only three weeks after he had died, it was difficult to celebrate. Even that soon after my father's death, I could feel the foundation of my relationship with my mother shifting, something I had not anticipated. I missed my father immeasurably, but her feelings seemed larger than life and required more attention, and it was difficult to balance the two. My father had always said, long before he became ill, "when I'm gone make sure you take care of your mother." I would try to brush it off, telling him that of course I would, but that he would probably outlive all of us. Now I was confronted with that task, in the face of my own heart breaking; and, in some confusing way, I felt angry. My sister and her children and I came together for my mother's birthday, trying to make it festive with cake and presents, but the elephant was in the room; the grief that frequently overtook us in quiet and not-so-quiet ways, reminding us that life was fleeting, and that things between us would never again be the same.

I remember many days in the months following my father's death that my sense of my physical self felt tenuous. I would think about losing him and my voice would catch or my chest would tighten, and it would feel difficult for me to catch my breath. I tried to remind myself to breathe through each moment, as I did when I meditated, knowing that what I was feeling would soon transmute into something else, something more manageable. It was at these times I would try to remember a funny story about my father. Once, many years before his death, I was away on vacation and sent my parents a fruit basket to cheer them up, as my mother had not been feeling well. I called to see if it had arrived safely, and my father had answered the phone. After a bit of chit-chat, I asked him what the fruit basket was like, expecting that perhaps he would say it was nice and that they were enjoying it. My father, however, in his inimitable way, started out, "Aaagh, the pears are lousy." That line became a signature for him in my mind, and even years later I would chuckle about it with friends who knew and loved him. In the dark moments after I lost him, it still brought a smile to my face when I thought of it—the bitter with the sweet.

I also struggled with the fact that everyday life continued, despite the enormity of this loss. A few weeks after my father died, I was driving on the highway in the late afternoon, directly facing a beautiful sunset. It was one of those red suns that you usually only see in the summer; the clouds were magenta and violet, and the air held those first subtle sweet smells of spring. I remember thinking, "How can this be?" I had just gone through one of the most intense experiences in my life, and the sun was setting, just like it always did. I was looking at it and realizing how incredibly beautiful it was and how lucky I was to see it. It was then that I realized that both experiences could in fact exist simultaneously—that I could be raging against the fact that I had just lost my father and I could find joy in this beautiful sunset. Ignoring the sunset would not make its beauty go away. Wishing my father alive again would not bring him back. Zen principles teach that suffering is an opportunity to awaken spiritually. It shows us our attachments, enables us to feel empathy for others, and helps us to develop the courage we need to continue living. In that moment, I had to let go of my attachment to wanting things to be different, knowing that if I didn't, it would keep me from my life. I heard my father's voice in my head, in the way I knew he would speak if he had seen the same sunset. I imagined him in the passenger's seat, looking out through the windshield with me, a slight smile on his face.

"Donna," he would sigh, "isn't this bee-YOU-ti-ful?"

CLINICAL CONSIDERATIONS AND APPLICATIONS

After considering such examples of an extended metaphor/activity for the processing of grief and the unveiling of meaning, we turn now to the clinical applications of grief work for both the general population and more specifically for Italian Americans. While the bereavement literature has discussed how grieving clients may be helped (Nadeau 2006; Worden 1982), there is no set formula as to how this should take place in the clinical encounter. As discussed above, the Italian American experience of grief may be considered deeper than in the dominant culture, owing to its lack of fear surrounding death (Boscia-Mulé 1999), the connection to mysticism and the afterlife, and the fact that drama, symbol, and ritual are important vehicles for life events, particularly regarding death. A family therapy model developed by the Milan group (Boscolo et al. 1987) attends to these nonlinear vehicles by basing itself on "circular questioning" and the use of ritual, which may be particularly salient to Italian American clients. The work of Boscolo et al. (1987) may be particularly applicable in the discussion of metaphor, with its emphasis on family meanings, the use of metaphorical objects to enter a family's shared myths, the transmission of messages that transcend the literal contents of a family's narrative, and, as Nadeau (2006) has suggested, the introduction of new information that can lead to new or revised family myths and accompanying interactions. Konigsberg (2011) has cited research that suggests that grief may follow a much more circuitous process; therefore, following proscribed stages may not be applicable to Italian or Italian American clients as they process their grief in psychotherapy. In light of the above context and available literature, we offer a number of suggestions to incorporate into clinical work with Italian or Italian American clients. These considerations, including the use of metaphor and the exploration of cultural rituals, will also be discussed as they apply to an Italian American client who sought therapy from one of the authors (DiCello). Throughout this discussion, details have been obscured to protect client confidentiality.

ASSESS THE GENERATIONAL POSITION OF THE CLIENT (E.G., FIRST, SECOND, OR THIRD GENERATION) AND THE LEVEL OF ACCULTURATION. For those clients who are first generation, for example, traditional rituals to exemplify mourning (e.g., wearing black clothing) may be considered more of a sign of respect than for a third-generation individual or for someone who has become much more Americanized.

ASK ABOUT RECENT AND PAST LOSSES. It is not uncommon for past losses to impact and influence more recent ones, particularly if the past losses have not been fully expressed and processed. In the Italian and Italian American family, familial ties are critical, and if there have been multiple family losses, the level of grief may become more complicated and extended. The meaning of past losses for the client should be explored.

ASK ABOUT THE FAMILIAL CONTEXT AT THE TIME OF THE LOSS. Were there other losses (e.g., financial) at the time of the death? Was there acrimony between family members at the time that impacted the grieving process? Was there the birth of a child at the time of the loss of an elder?

VIEW GRIEF AS A PROCESS, NOT PATHOLOGY. In Western culture, there can be a sanitized approach to death and the connection to the loved one. Cultural rituals that may be viewed as odd (e.g., keeping a shrine to the deceased) should be validated and explored as to the meaning for the client. The bonds to the deceased (e.g., what might need to be relinquished and what can be continued) should also be considered.

ALLOW FOR AND EVEN ENCOURAGE THE POSSIBILITY OF GRIEVING THROUGH AN EXTENDED METAPHOR. Clients may find something meaningful that they can do over time that connects them to the deceased in an ongoing, healthy way and helps them to work through the painful aspects of the relationship and the loss.

USE THE DECEASED IN PSYCHOTHERAPY. If the bond with the deceased was positive, and there is not a contraindication in doing so, questions such as "What would (name of the deceased person) say about this?" may be helpful to the client in processing his or her grief and remaining connected to the deceased in a positive way. The use of such questions may be comforting to the bereaved and indicate validation on the part of the therapist to the client's relationship with the deceased and to his or her experience of grieving.

USE CIRCULAR QUESTIONING REGARDING OTHERS' PERCEPTIONS OF THE CLIENT'S GRIEVING PROCESS. As previously indicated, the use of circular questioning has been found to be beneficial in working with Italian and Italian American clients in particular. Questions, such as the following, validate the client's connection to family and can give the therapist insight into how the client's grieving process is being viewed in a larger context: Who is the most upset in your family about this loss? Who in your family has had the strongest reaction to this death? The least? What might be the role you, or others, play in the family in terms of holding the grief or letting it go?

INQUIRE ABOUT THE CLIENT'S DREAMS OF THE DECEASED. If the client has had dreams about the deceased, such dreams may be rich with symbolism and may be a window into the use of metaphor. For some clients, it can be helpful to take these dreams literally as visitations with the dead; interpreting their meaning could move one further away from the grief or the deceased.

CASE VIGNETTE

Anne (a pseudonym) was a fifty-six-year-old Italian American woman who was referred to psychotherapy by her daughter. Anne described her daughter as stating, "My mother is going crazy," based on her perception of Anne's "prolonged" grieving of her mother's death. Anne presented with a self-described long-standing depression and stated in her initial session that "I can't let go of my kids." She was willing to begin treatment in order "to feel less depressed" and "to understand why I took my mother's death so hard."

Anne had a high school education and had been married for thirty years to a man who she claims "I now have nothing in common with." She has a thirty-two-year-old daughter and a thirty-four-year-old son; the daughter is single with two children, and the son is married with one child and "is my perfect child." Anne's parents emigrated to the United States from Italy at the turn of the century, with all four of their children having been born in the United States. Anne is the youngest of the siblings, with an older sister and two older brothers. From Anne's description, it was a lively Italian family, with traditional Sunday dinners, lots of banter and opinions, and traditional gender roles. Anne's father had died ten years previously, and she described having a close relationship with him. Her mother had died a year prior to her beginning treatment, and she stated, "I just can't face the fact that she died; I don't think she is gone." From Anne's description, her mother was very involved in Anne's family, often offering unsolicited advice to Anne regarding the raising of her own children. Despite the fact that Anne had three other siblings, anytime her mother needed something, she would call Anne—often two to three times a day. Anne was also the primary caretaker for her mother in the months preceding her death and oversaw all of the funeral arrangements. Anne described being angry at her mother for dying, and stated, "I feel like she left me when I needed her; my kid's lives are a mess, now I have no one to talk to about it."

I was very interested in hearing Anne's perceptions of her daughter's views regarding Anne's grieving for her mother. Anne stated that she didn't feel that it was excessive; she went to the cemetery at least five times a week, often staying for half an hour to "talk" with her mother. She also went on major holidays, leaving flowers or holiday cards at the gravesite. When asked her thoughts about why her daughter was so concerned about this, she stated: "My daughter, she's too American; you can hardly tell that she is Italian. She never comes for Sunday dinner any longer, only calls me once a week, she has no connection to the things I did with my mother." This brought tears to her eyes, but it was clearly the connection with her mother that was generating the sadness, not the fact that her daughter had become Americanized. I asked Anne what she thought her mother would have to say about her granddaughter. Anne laughed and said, "She would have a *lot* to say. She'd say that that is why Angela's [also a pseudonym] life is so messed up, she doesn't follow tradition. Her older son has trouble in school, her baby's father takes off all the time, she's depressed herself." I then asked Anne what advice her mother might have for her as she watched her daughter struggle: "'Don't get mad at her,' but that's so hard to do." Anne then remarked that she never thought about actually "talking" to her mother about Angela, but now maybe she would the next time she went to the cemetery; she remarked: "It feels good to think about what my mother would actually say to me." I also thought it important that I not comment on her going to the cemetery in an attempt to normalize it, given her daughter's perceptions and the fact that I was not yet certain what it meant to her.

At the second session, Anne timidly asked what I thought about her daughter's comments that she was "going crazy" because she went to the cemetery so frequently. I told her that while I also wanted to explore more of what going to the cemetery meant to her, I thought that it was a way for her to stay connected to her mother and that she must have been very attached to her. Anne visibly relaxed at this and went on to discuss how she almost felt "driven" to get to the cemetery as much as she could, "like people who wash their hands all the time." As we explored this over a number of sessions, the conflicted feelings that Anne had for her mother became apparent and were gently explored. About four months into her therapy, Anne described her feelings of grief in a very metaphorical way: "Sometimes when I think about my mother, it feels like a tidal wave washing over me, and I can't breathe." This metaphor led us to explore the feelings of suffocation that Anne often felt with her mother; how her mother "took up a lot of space, in my head and in my life." Anne felt extremely guilty about feeling this way and often cried in session after expressing these feelings. Concurrently, she also reported feeling less depressed in her daily life during this time, much less focused on her daughter, and was only going to the cemetery twice a week. When I asked Anne to consider how talking about the "tidal wave" and feeling better might be connected, she replied: "It's the tidal wave; when my mother was alive, she was always in my business, but I could never tell her it was too much, I just took it like a good daughter. Now that she's gone, I can talk about what it felt like, how sometimes I wanted to scream; and I started to do that to my daughter. I loved my mother, but sometimes she was a pain in the a**." Both Anne and I came to understand her need to go to the cemetery as somewhat of a reaction formation to the feelings she could not deal with while her mother was alive. On her next visit to the cemetery, Anne reported that she was able to "tell" her mother some of this. I asked her how her mother "took" it. She began laughing and said, "I can't repeat it!" When I asked Anne if she felt like she was going to the cemetery enough, she replied: "For right now, I am. But I know that if I feel like I need to go more often, I will, but not out of guilt. I'll just want to be close to her."

Anne remained in therapy for approximately eighteen months, so the above vignette only gives a small glimpse into our work together. Though she never addressed other salient therapy issues (such as being in a relatively unhappy marriage and enabling some of her daughter's unwise decisions), she left therapy feeling less depressed and feeling more in control about how she processed and managed her grief surrounding her mother's death. Toward the end of her therapy, she reported the following dream: "I am cooking in the kitchen, and the phone is ringing. I know that it is my mother. I pick up the phone and tell her that I can't talk right now, that I am busy and will call her later. She starts arguing with me in Italian and tells me that I'm a 'no good daughter.' I smile to myself and tell her I love her and hang up the phone." As Anne narrated the dream, she was overcome with emotion. The meaning, evident to both Anne and me, was a clear sign that Anne had taken control, even in death, of her relationship with her mother. When I asked Anne what brought the tears to the surface, after a moment she replied: "It was really strange; as I finished telling you the dream, I felt both the love I have for my mother, still, and the parts that made me unhappy with her at the same time—and it was OK." In processing her comment, Anne came to acknowledge that there were a number of variables that contributed to this realization: We kept her mother an active presence in her therapy; we depathologized the rituals that were culturally important to her (e.g., visiting the cemetery); and we explored the metaphors and dreams that Anne brought into the therapy. In her last session, I asked Anne how she might deal with the "tidal wave" if it appeared in the future, either in relationship to her mother or with someone else. She thought for a moment and said: "What was that phrase you told me once, 'You can't stop the waves but you can learn to surf?' I guess I'm surfing."

CONCLUSIONS

This essay is meant to highlight a number of issues related to Italian and Italian American conceptualizations of grief. Despite examining other cultures, the psychological literature has not addressed the possibility that Italian American culture and ritual can contribute to Western conceptualizations of grief; we propose that there are inherent cultural themes that may inform clinical work with Italian Americans and broaden Western conceptualizations. We also propose a number of determinants to consider when working clinically with Italian American clients who are contending with loss. One of the most salient is the use of metaphor, which the literature has discussed as a way for therapists to aid clients in making meaning of their loss and of their experiences with the grieving process, and which may be particularly helpful with the Italian American population. In addition, metaphors may allow for a new understanding of grief as a difficult process and allow healing in a more comprehensive way. Following the deaths of our fathers, we both used metaphor as a way to deal with the healing process and meaning making of our loss and have included brief excerpts of our own experiences in the discussion here. Finally, the case vignette of an Italian American client offers a comprehensive way to understand the direct application of this proposed material.

Grief and mourning are certainly very individual experiences and can take many directions when they arise in the clinical encounter. As in Anne's situation, grief transmutes over time, and what a client might need immediately after a loss might not be the same as months or years later. It is our belief that depathologizing and validating many of the rituals and beliefs in Italian American culture can bring grieving to a deeper level, central to each individual client and to mainstream culture at large. Each story of grief, intimate and personal, reinforces "the fact that relationships change but do not end after death" (Bona 2010, 208) and, as

Frasca (2008) has demonstrated in the poem that opens this chapter, may even evolve in our dreams.

References

Alba, Richard. 2000. "The Twilight of Ethnicity among Americans of European Ancestry: The Case of the Italians." In *The Review of Italian American Studies*, edited by Frank M. Sorrentino and Jerome Krase, 41–74. Lanham, MD: Lexington Books.

Barreca, Regina. 2002. "Preface: Special Issue on Italian American Literature." *LIT: Literature Interpretation Theory* 13(3):167–171.

Bayor, Ronald H. 2009. "Another Look at 'Whiteness': The Persistence of Ethnicity in American Life." *Journal of American Ethnic History* 29(1):13–30.

Berlin, Richard M., Mary E. Olson, Carlos E. Cano, and Susan Engel. 1991. "Metaphor and Psychotherapy." *American Journal of Psychotherapy* 35(3):359–367.

Bona, Mary Jo. 2010. *By the Breaths of Their Mouths: Narratives of Resistance in Italian America*. Albany, NY: SUNY Press.

Boscia-Mulé, Patricia. 1999. *Authentic Ethnicities: The Interaction of Ideology, Gender Power, and Class in the Italian American Experience*. Westport, CT: Greenwood Press.

Boscolo, Luigi, Gianfranco Cecchin, Lynn Hoffman, and Peggy Penn. 1987. *Milan Systemic Family Therapy*. New York: Basic Books.

Frasca, Maria. 2008. "The Visit." *Arba Sicula*. 29(1 & 2):25–31.

Gambino, Richard. 1997. "The Crisis of Italian American Identity." In *Beyond the Godfather: Italian American Writers on the Real Italian American Experience*, edited by A. Kenneth Ciongoli and Jay Parini, 269–288. Hanover, NH: University Press of New England.

Giordano, Joe, Monica McGoldrick, and Joanne Guarino Klages. 2005. "Italian Families." In *Ethnicity and Family Therapy*, 3rd ed., edited by Monica McGoldrick, Joe Giordano, and Nydia Garcia-Preto, 616–628, New York: Guilford Press.

Guglielmo, Jennifer. 2003. "Introduction: White Lies, Dark Truths." *Are Italians White?: How Race Is Made in America*, edited by Jennifer Guglielmo and Salvatore Salerno, 1–16. New York: Routledge.

Konigsberg, Ruth D. 2011. *The Truth about Grief: The Myth of Its Five Stages and the New Science of Loss*. New York: Simon & Schuster.

Lakoff, George, and Mark Johnson. 1980. *Metaphors We Live By*. Chicago: University of Chicago Press.

Luconi, Stefano. 2004. "Becoming Italian in the US: Through the Lens of Life Narratives." 2004. *MELUS* 29(3/4):151–164.

Mangione, Jerre, and Ben Morreale. 1992. *La Storia: Five Centuries of the Italian American Experience*. New York: Harper Perrenial.

Nadeau, Janice W. 2006. "Metaphorically Speaking: The Use of Metaphors in Grief Therapy." *Illness, Crisis & Loss* 14(3):201–221.

Rosenblatt, Paul C. 2008. "Grief across Cultures: A Review and Research Agenda." In *Handbook of Bereavement Research and Practice: Advances in Theory and Intervention*, edited by Margaret S. Stroebe, Robert O. Hansson, Henk Schut, and Wolfgang Stroebe, 207–222. Washington, DC: American Psychological Association.

Siegelman, Ellen. 1993. *Metaphor and Meaning in Psychotherapy*. New York: Guilford Press.

Stanford Artificial Intelligence Laboratory. 2011. "Literary Terms." Accessed April 10: http://ai.stanford.edu/~csewell/culture/litterms.htm.

Vecoli, Rudolph J. 2000. "Are Italian Americans just White Folks?" *The Review of Italian American Studies*, edited by Frank M. Sorrentino and Jerome Krase, 75–88. Lanham, MD: Lexington Books.

Worden, J. William. 1982. *Grief Counseling and Grief Therapy*. New York: Springer.

Italian American Women's Poetry and Identity Development: Suggestions for Working with Italian American Women and Issues of Identity

LORRAINE MANGIONE
RACHEL MCBRIDE

INTRODUCTION: ITALIAN AMERICAN WOMEN AND IDENTITY

Who am I as an Italian, an American, and a woman? What is my relationship to being Italian, to heritage and immigration, and to family, and how does that influence who I am as a person? These and other questions of identity for Italian American women, explored through the lens of poetry, are the subject matter of this essay. Questions of identity for anyone in contemporary American culture are significant, for identity is not just handed down to us as it might have been in more traditional, stable times (McWilliams 1999). Ethnic identity development tends to elicit more questions and ambiguities, for it implies some juggling of more than one identity or transforming from one identity to another and that relationship to the dominant culture. [See Phinney (1996) or Arredondo et al. (1996) for more of a discussion of identity, ethnicity, and other variables.] Writers on Italian ethnic identity from sociology, ethnic studies, and literary studies have discussed issues of stereotyping, the role and importance of ethnicity, and the question of Italian Americans' place in the range of immigrant groups in this country (Bayor 2009; Barreca 2002; Gambino 1997; Luconi 2004; Alba 2000; Vecoli 2000). Women's identity in the twentieth century adds another layer of complexity, as the changing roles and images of women have in turn transformed the ways women think about who they are, their sense of self, and their possibilities, which intersects with how Italian American women have and have not created an identity (Albright and Moore 2011; Messina 1994; Barolini 1985). Identity development does not happen in a vacuum but is a complex process involving the individual and the context. The mainstream media would hand us a range of images of Italian American women across the age and acculturation cohorts, yet some of these are worn-out and superficial images of identity, while others feel stuck in a time warp. We propose that there is more nuance, depth, and variation in paths of identity development taken by Italian American women, while at the same time common issues or themes can resonate across women. In this essay, we explore identity development in Italian American women by looking at a sampling of poetry and considering its messages about identity.

WHY POETRY?

Poetry was chosen partly because Italian American women have found their poetry voices and have written a substantial amount of poetry, particularly in the last sixty or so years. Looking deeply at poets, or at any artist perhaps, is a way of seeing a particular process enlarged, like using a magnifying glass. We suggest that poets can thereby show us something about the issue of identity development, a major human task that would certainly show up in poetry. Poetry allows the stepping further into a psychological issue, yet also stepping back to write one's poem. To create is to have an outlet and a voice, a way to foster something in yourself and in others. Thus, the hope is that poets with their voices will express a process that occurs in others who do not have a voice to express or describe it. Poetry, through its use of metaphorical language and symbolic thought, can also access the more unconscious aspects of self and identity and offer clues as to what processes and dynamics out of awareness might be important to Italian American women and identity formation. We see poetry as expressing something about Italian American women and identity but also as helping the poet in creating or developing her identity, which leads to the following questions: What does this poem express about identity? How is poetry used in developing one's identity? Our criterion in choosing the specific poems to discuss are poems that seemed to announce themselves to us, in our perusal (by no means exhaustive, partly due to the difficulty of accessing smaller poetry and literary magazines) of poetry by Italian American women from about the midtwentieth century to the present time, as having something profound to do with identity formation. We are not writing as literary critics, nor to analyze the individual women poets, but rather we are looking at the poetry as psychological documents that can teach us about identity.

THEORETICAL PERSPECTIVES ON IDENTITY FORMATION
AND DEVELOPMENT OF THE SELF

Three streams of psychological thought frame our work. The first is object relations theories with an emphasis on Winnicott (1971) and the development of cultural contribution as "the third." The concept of the third is a representation of where creativity occurs: A symbolic space that represents the interplay between a person's inner life and the outer world. Erikson (1963) and Erikson and Erikson (1997) and life span development is the second stream, particularly their thinking about identity formation as well as the later stages of Generativity versus Stagnation and Ego Integrity versus Despair. The final stream is Falicov's (1995) parameters of culture, which lend texture to the immigration and acculturation experience. Below are brief descriptions of each area, which will later be integrated into the discussion of the poetry itself.

OBJECT RELATIONS. Winnicott (1971) wrote of cultural experiencing as a type of play, with its earliest origins occurring in infant–mother relations. When mother provides for the child's creative experiencing, the baby is able to use objects creatively. The same process occurs in all creative endeavors; one uses both that which already exists (language, culture) and yet constructs something that is personal and creative (the poem). Because art is closely tied to culture, developmental deficits in artistic expression suggest difficulties shared by the culture at large. Poems carry within them the losses or deprivations experienced by a culture. If the baby does not have the space to play, then "it follows there is no link with the cultural inheritance, and there will be no contribution to the cultural pool" (Winnicott 1971, 137). The ability to create is then hindered; or worse, objects that are not one's own become inserted and lead to a "false self" (Winnicott 1971, 137). As Italian caricatures abound in American culture, complex representations of Italian Americans are difficult to find. Italian American poetry has not achieved the literary acclaim that other ethnicities have achieved. Italian American poets are thus giving language to a culture that cannot find its self in the cultural sphere, and they are left vulnerable to impinging representations leading to false identities.

LIFE SPAN DEVELOPMENT. Identity formation, although a separate stage in Erikson's life span development framework, can also be seen as the cornerstone of his work and as pervading all of the stages. It certainly seems that identity is reworked many times throughout life, even if something basic and fundamental is consolidated in the earlier years. The reworking of identity in later years is central to the discussion of a woman who started writing poetry at age eighty. Some of the challenges during this later stage of life are issues around relationship to the generations coming after one, seen in the tension of Generativity versus Stagnation, where generativity is defined as "the concern in establishing and guiding the next generation" (Erikson 1963, 267). Questions around this stage include the following: Does the person resign and stagnate as he or she gets older, turning away from the next generation, or does a person find meaning in giving to and engaging with the next generation in a way that honors his or her learning, perspective, and wisdom? Other challenges come to the surface as an older person reflects on his or her life and comes to some sense of either ego integrity and wholeness or despair and fragmentation, seen in the tension of Ego Integrity versus Despair. Has one had a good enough life, have the choices and experiences been, on the whole, ones that have given meaning to life? Or, does one feel the despair of regret and loss? These are themes that animate the poet's work presented here.

CULTURE AND ACCULTURATION. Finally, parameters of culture and acculturation (Falicov 1995) and how they might interact with identity development are noted, as they seem crucial to understanding identity and ethnicity. These include (378):

1. Ecological Context: Diversity in where and how the family lives and how it fits in its environment.
2. Migration and Acculturation: Diversity in where the family members came from; when, how, and why; how they live; and their future aspirations.
3. Family Organization: Diversity in the preferred forms of cultural family organization and the values connected to those family arrangements.
4. Family Life Cycle: Diversity in how developmental stages and transitions in the family life cycle are culturally patterned.

THE PRESENT INQUIRY

The purpose of this essay is to consider and respond to these questions of identity: What is important for/in the creation and evolution of identity of an Italian American woman? What are the issues, conflicts, strengths, values, and experiences that might make up her identity? How can this study of poetry help us to understand and work with other Italian American women who may have struggles and questions around identity development?

In the next two sections, we offer an in-depth look at poetry and identity development. The first examines poetry from a couple of sources through the psychodynamic, object relations lens described above. A theory of loss and mourning is presented as central to Italian American women and identity development. In the second section, one poet's work is explored through the lens of life span development and acculturation. Themes of life review, giving to others, one's relationship to acculturation, and ongoing intimacy with loved ones are salient.

In the final section, suggestions stemming from our study of Italian American women poets that might help mental health professionals in working with other Italian American women are noted. A particular focus is the twin themes of loss and resiliency that can be found in the poetry described in the chapter and that are so often prominent in the lives and identities of an immigrant population.

NARRATIVES ABOUT POETRY AND IDENTITY DEVELOPMENT

THE HOLLOW INHERITENCE: ABSENCE, MOURNING, AND DISCOVERY

In MTV's reality show, *Jersey Shore*, young Italian Americans call each other "wop" and "Guido." Many were outraged at the stereotypes portrayed in the show. The network got death threats. UNICO (an Italian American service organization) president Andre Dimino told *The New York Times*: "Their behavior is reprehensible and demeaning in all respects. I don't see any redeeming value in the show. They are an embarrassment to themselves and to their families" (Eisinger 2009).

What Dimino did not mention was that they were an embarrassment to us—to Italian Americans. It is a shame that comes from identification. One threatens a caricature or stereotype only when one's own annihilation terror has signaled a threat. If we awaken in the night and shoot our own shadow, it is because we were not so certain that it was a shadow. Rage seems to conceal the more difficult, shakier question. Just at the point that we yell, "I am not that" (as adolescents frequently do when in the throes of forging an identity), there may be a question that is not allowed to break through to the surface. It is the sad and hungry, the empty and searching, open mouthed whisper of "what am I?" It is the fuel behind the fire—blatant as one of the *Jersey Shore* character's Italian flag tattoos. Flags are erected to ensure ownership and assert boundaries. It is as if the Italian American skin is too permeable. We must put flags on our bodies and rage at stereotypes because we have some collective sense that our skin is a thirsty one—a skin that may let anything in. For that matter, who is there to let in? It is difficult to find complex Italian figures within the culture, and the absence speaks volumes. The absence is present in the poetry of Italian American women who seem to be expressing something of what has been left out of cultural experience. While Italians have successfully navigated much of American society, they have fallen short in their attempt to create a cultural identity for themselves. Pellegrino D'Acierno [as cited in Barolini (1985)] notes that Italians have failed to utilize duality (and thus bicultural identity) to foster artistic expression. The American dream was swallowed whole, which lends danger to the flat and ridiculous stereotypes and the cartoonish shadows in the cultural mirror.

The works of Winnicott (1971) and Green (1980/2001) are used as a framework to understand cultural experience in general and to explore the meaning absence has as it manifests in the cultural contribution. Italian American women's poetry can be used to understand how Mother-Italy's American children have been left with a shadow and emptiness in regard to their own identity. Poetry also indicates the ways Italian Americans can give birth to a culture that fills in the shadowy gaps.

Winnicott (1971) writes of cultural experience and contribution as the "third," initially appearing in transitional phenomena. When conditions allow, the baby begins to use objects as symbols of "me" and "not me," creations that are representative of a play space that is not solely imaginative, nor solely objective. It is the basis of imagination and contains within it a type of merging at the point of separation. Winnicott writes that the "interplay between originality and the acceptance of tradition as the basis for inventiveness seems to be just one more example, and a very exciting one, of the interplay between separateness and union" (134).

Things can go wrong. When there is a loss of object during an early age, a diminished ability to use the play space ensues. If the infant cannot depend on the availability of the mother, then loss of meaningful play will result. The intermediate area where play occurs can be cluttered with objects that are not of the infant's creative force but injected into the space by something externally; for instance, the *Jersey Shore* characters, *The Godfather* movies, and the like. This cannot happen unless deprivation has already created the vulnerability. Andre Green's (1980/2001) concept of the dead mother refers to:

> An imago which has been constituted in the child's mind, following a maternal depression, brutally transforming a living object, which was a source of vitality for the child, into a distant figure, toneless, practically inanimate, deeply impregnating the cathexis of certain patients . . . and weighing on the destiny of their object-libidinal and narcissistic future . . . [The] dead mother, is a mother who remains alive but who is, so to speak, psychically dead in the eyes of the child in her care. (142)

The child identifies with the absence and takes the absence within to have a relationship with it. Some poets are able to comment on the absence. They seem to be able to use objects to represent the deadness, indicating that they have begun to work through the identification. Others are unable to comment upon the dilemma directly, and the poem leaves the reader with a sense of flatness/hollowness. It is these poems that seem to be possessed with a firmer allegiance to the object: They will love nothing else but what was kept from them. For Italian Americans, this may have meant the idea of the old country (preventing a bicultural identity). Finally, a few poets are able to speak not only about the deadness but also convey the mourning to accompany it. They have somehow managed to give up the identification with that which was made unavailable to them. Life and passion are found in the poems. Poets thus pave a developmental pathway toward utilizing the play space . . . from identification, to observing capacity, to mourning.

Poetry can help us to understand what has gone wrong in the cultural play space for Italian Americans. Idealization/wish fulfillment, hollowness and absence, and loss and mourning arise as themes among the poetry.

"Naturally, Mother," by Janine Veto (Barolini 1985), shows the allegiance to a mother who has become a love-object at the expense of others:

> But you were always with me
> every time I loved and left
> each time I put my life in suitcases
> as I watch the coupling of friends
> and know I cannot follow. (341)

She explains that "a woman bleeds through her mother" (342). She speaks here of identification. It is the sameness and the merger of womanhood. A woman's blood is also proof that she has not conceived. The speaker in the poem will not be coupled like her friends, and perhaps this is evidence that her love for her mother, who is present in the poem only through her absence, is the only love she will allow. In the dead mother complex, pleasure is forbidden. "Behind the dead mother complex, behind the blank mourning for the mother, one catches a glimpse of the mad passion of which she is, and remains, the object, that renders mourning for her an impossible experience" (Green, 1980/2001, 162). In "Body Wisdom," Veto (Barolini 1985) writes that

> we come
> out of unknown bodies
> our own and its opposite
> alien as first breath
> grappling on the grave of wonder. (340–341)

In Winnicott's (1971) metaphor, the mother's body is the ocean and the space between is the shore. For Veto, it is a grave.

In "Back in the Old Country" (Barolini 1985), the reader is taken on a trip to the mother country with Anne Paolucci. The poem begins with her fantasy of what she would be like if she were a simple Italian girl in her father's village. The poem then shifts to her real experience in her voyage to the old country. The poem has a hollowness and dreamlike quality in it. It is as if both of Paolucci's versions of Italy are fantastical. It is difficult to know whose Italy Paolucci is visiting, both in her mind and on her real trip. It is as if she is taking the reader on the fantasized trip to the part of her unavailable mother. It has the static, embalmed quality of a snow globe:

> Back in that other world,
> I might have been a country girl, singing my mornings
> To the fountain's tune, carrying a pail
> Of water effortlessly on my head. (313)

Here, the love-object is Mother-Italy. If Italians were indeed "birds of passage," never intending to settle permanently in the new country, their eyes were always tilted a bit toward home. A child is an accidental root in the soil. It is not difficult to imagine that immigrants, always intending to go back home, had not mourned the loss of their own Mother-Italy. The idea of home could have taken on its own sad encapsulated space in the mother and left children hungering for identification with this part. Paolucci describes nostalgia in her eyes that may hold the fantasy that if one could only reach the unreachable, could walk in the land of the undead dead, they could be embraced as one of them, "among my people" (314). It is a sad predicament, a holding on to an unavailable frozen-over conceptualization of Italy that prevents a bicultural identity from flourishing.

In "Italian Bread" (Barolini 1985), Kathy Freeperson experiences her hunger as being forced upon her. Bread is a "monster" and there are "Italian bread pushers." She speaks both of absence and swallowing it whole, against one's own better judgment. The experience of having the transitional space cluttered with objects from the outside is present in the "pushing" of the bread. Here, it seems as if instead of identification and internalization of a dead mother, the absence is forced upon her:

Exorcize the little Italian
Devil who makes fat and
Mucus.
As grandma and ma
Shove it towards me. (303)
Furthermore:
This loaf has a (w)hole like a
mouth saying "oh"
like the tongue's response
when it hits slice
after slice
the hole continues
but in a little different size
dunked in gravies, juices
it gets sloppy drunk and
wavers before the
open mouth bent close to
receive it.
Soggy with the taste of whatever
Else is served. (304)

Although Freeperson loses the fight against her hunger for the bread, her anger at the hunger that exists for the "(w)hole" is promising. If one identifies and becomes the absent part of their parent, several things are accomplished. Most importantly, one does not have to mourn the loss of the mother. The parts of her from which the child was shut out (including the conceptualization of the mother culture) are internal and within psychic reach. But the half-dead have a difficult time at playing. If one is one's mother, and one's unavailable mother at that, there is little room to grow into oneself. In "The Light of Fallen Stars," Sylvia Forges Ryan (2008) is mourning the loss of her Italian father and embarks on a search to understand who he was. In doing this, she is separate. She has not merged with an unavailable person. Ryan speaks of her mourning and also the literal experience of growing up with one deceased parent. Here, she paves the way for what other Italian Americans must do. If absence is swallowed whole, little bicultural identity can form. Poems are hollow, Italy is idealized or unacknowledged, and food becomes the only cultural link (the earliest and most simplistic connection to the mother). Ryan's poem is complex and alive . . . because she is able to mourn. Ryan speaks of her childhood experience with her mourning mother:

> But just a shred
> now and then was all she'd
> share with me. And I,
> desperate not to see
> her sorrow, learned to conspire
> with her, trying to save us two.

Ryan seeks a third component outside of her conspiracy with her mother, concretely in her father and metaphorically in the cultural sphere of poetry. She searches for her father's passion in adult life and finds bits and pieces of him. Her attempt to know him and his Italianness, his passion, his life, is her attempt to move beyond deadness. She grapples for what was never there to be given. She seems to come up from the water gasping for life, and her father is seen in her through these attempts. If Mother-Italy was not shared with the later generations of Italian Americans because of our ancestors' sorrow, the journey toward identity is first with absence, then mourning, and, finally, discovery. Ryan (2008) leads the way:

A glint of insight and I begin to get
how all these pieces fit, more
how what seemed most lost
was mostly near, salvaged
waiting to lead me in and through
as one finds direction
by the light of fallen stars
that still shine on and on
making words, things, names, new.

BECOMING A POET AT AGE EIGHTY

It is as if the poet Josephine Geluso is stepping back and looking at a grand Italian mosaic, like the ones one might find in Piazza Armerina on the island of Sicily, the birthplace of Geluso's parents. In this mosaic, one sees the progression of Geluso's life from childhood in New York with her family of origin, young adulthood, marriage and raising children, adulthood, and, finally, herself growing older. Intertwined with this retrospective are: Topics of heritage and tradition; transition to this country and transitions within this country; food and its cooking, sharing, growing, and relationship to family; spirituality (which seems to connect with nature and a strong sense of place); death and loss; missed opportunities; and gratefulness. Woven throughout is the theme of identity, of who she is, as she looks back, consolidates her sense of self, connects with her past and, particularly, her extended family (but stays alive to the present), explores who she is as an Italian, and looks at herself getting older. The identity themes are in the process of the poetry writing as she looks over her life as well as the content: Family/childhood, being Italian, and aging. In reading her poetry, one gets the sense of Geluso observing and feeling the intricate mosaic of her life and self, with some humor and awareness of the poignancy of exploring and summing up a life in one's eighties, and with great arms that can hold and contain a lifetime of joy and heartache. The bits of humor and the moments of poignancy seem to create some space for her to step back and take stock. Falicov's (1995) ideas about culture and family, and Erikson's (1963) ideas about identity and the last two stages of his life span development, come alive in these poems. After a brief note as to how Geluso was selected for inclusion here, this essay explores five of her poems with regard to identity development.

Geluso was introduced to one of the authors in the best Italian tradition of community and family—through Geluso's niece, who was a friend of the author. Geluso's niece was a psychologist, an expert in trauma who had then become a Jungian, and, thus, was keenly attuned to reintegration of childhood memories, meaning-making, archetypes, and symbols—all potential aspects of poetry. The idea of becoming a poet at age eighty was intriguing to the author, who then followed Geluso's career and poetry. Her work seemed a natural fit for this discussion.

Five poems or sets of poems have been chosen for discussion because they represent the identity themes described above of being Italian, family/childhood, and aging. The first three poems were also chosen because they speak of the parameters of emigration and immigration. These poems represent the old country, the voyage to America, and the changes involved in living in the new world. Geluso's story is situated in a certain time and place—the great southern Italian migration to the United States, specifically New York City in the early twentieth century, and, as such, reflects that world and those experiences. The fourth poem finds her and her family squarely in the middle of the new world, creating a life in America. The last set of poems speaks of her life right now—a woman in her eighties looking at her life and herself. In a sense, all of these poems might be addressing the following questions, questions that could be asked by many immigrants or by anyone wishing to understand themselves: Who am I (or we)? Where do I (or we) come from? How have I (or we) grown and changed?

"SICILIAN STORYTELLER" OR MY GRANDFATHER AND I. In "Sicilian Storyteller" (Geluso 2003), the poet's grandfather is evoked, and the poet is four years old, listening to her grandfather weave stories from his beloved Caltabellotta. Both the storyteller and the listener in the poem, as well as the reader, are whisked off to the land of his childhood, climbing through ruins, watching the shepherds with their jugs of milk, walking past fields of fruit, and tasting the olive oil. The oral tradition, so important in Italian culture and families, is alive and vibrant between this little girl and her grandfather, as he painted pictures for her to not only see but also feel. The feel of the poem is monumental—this was important material for Grandpa to be handing down. He was sharing the Italian heritage, and the little girl, so many years later, still has it within her. Along with descriptions of the land and mountains and people is this particularly mischievous image of Grandpa as a boy:

He glowed when he told
how he stole chunks of bread
to dip in the olive oil
stored in huge crocks,
aromatic green liquid
carefully pressed,
a treasure
not to be squandered by him. (27)

What is the treasure that the young girl, later poet, is not to squander? What is her aromatic green liquid to be protected? It certainly seems that she is to listen well, keep this world alive, and pass it on to the next generation. She promises herself in the end that she will keep the stories alive, "the cycle not to be broken by me" (27), and tell them to her children and grandchildren. She even promises she will go to Persephone's island and bring Grandpa back with her. It is as if the cycle will then be complete, with Grandpa in his homeland, and the images, tastes, smells, and people of Sicily passed down through the generations.

In Geluso's work we see how important it is, indeed, to keep the Old World alive and, for some, to make that return trip. It is an intimate part of who she is. We all come from there.

"THE EXCHANGE" OR ONE WORLD FOR ANOTHER. "The Exchange" (Geluso 2007) tells the story of the hardships and sorrows of emigration as a young woman in Italy is left behind when her husband goes to America for work. She has to fend for herself and does so by moving back with her family and running the exchange, where goods are bartered and food, such as fish, is traded for provolone. In the final stanza, we see the sorrow, the unknown, and the mystery, as "her Papa grieved" (21) when she left their "sun-soaked" (21) town for the mysteries of the new world. Here is the movement, the migration, told simply and with reference to food and family. We are left with our own questions — what would she find in the new world? Would there be exchanges where people met? Would there be family and food? How can one leave the family behind? What is the biggest exchange immigrants do? — one life and one world for something radically different, something unknown except for a few pictures, stories, or letters.

"EVOLUTION OF A SANDWICH" OR HOW TO BECOME AN AMERICAN. This poem both directly and metaphorically tells the story of acculturation

(Geluso, 2003). A child starts school with a frittata for lunch (and several other tasty Italian dishes), which evolves over time into a Wonder Bread American sandwich. We see the innocence, and what might now be hailed as "cultural diversity" in the child's lunch, how it evolves over time, and the desire to please the American teacher (who has other ideas about a proper lunch), and, thus, individual culture is obliterated. Is this how the famous melting pot melted?

One has to ask, what else changed besides the sandwich? What else was wiped away and replaced by Wonder Bread? How did the girl, her grandmother, and parents acclimate to a new culture inside themselves — what did they give up and what did they retain, and what was transformed into a new self and a new self-image? What happens to the "frittata" part of the child when she is asked to leave that behind?

"AND TWO DOGS" OR OUR LIFE IN BROOKLYN. Geluso writes many poems that capture the world of family in New York City in the first half of the twentieth century, peopled with her parents, grandparents, sister, and any number of extended family and neighbors. The tones are ones of longing, appreciation, sadness, wonder, and what seems like pure enjoyment of the memories evoked. In "And Two Dogs" (Geluso 2005), one is almost eavesdropping on the past and can hear the animated conversation and heated debates over Roosevelt for the men and bobbed hair for the women, listen to the kids at play on a player piano that must be magic, and take in the Sicilian ("passionate") and English ("temperate") mixture that swirled around them. The presence of the two dogs barking at the end serves to remind us of just how ordinary and normal this scene was, as well as, perhaps, the duality that exists in any immigrant's new life. The reader shares an intimate but ordinary moment in the life of an Italian family in Brooklyn, a family that is assimilating into the dominant culture but retains its old world ethos and flavor. The writer opens up her world to us with clarity and simplicity, it feels unadorned and honest. We are reminded of the role of conversation, debate, music, and just being together in people's lives before wealth, gadgets, cars, television, and texting.

"EIGHTY-SIX SUMMERS" OR SUMMING IT ALL UP. The last four poems in her last book, *If There's Music I Dance* (2007), all focus directly on issues of aging, life review, who she is now, what it means to be at this point in her life, her legacy, a sense of wisdom and learning, what might come next, and how she will enter into whatever comes next. There is a sense of peace and pride about who she is, her life, and how she has lived her life.

Even as she writes about aging she declares, "I'll never be old" ("Mere Years") because of her deep connection to her childhood. She is grateful for her eighty-six summers that have, of course, "flown by" as this poem also flies by, ranging from childhood years to the coming of death at her doorway. One sees the humor again, a sense of peace, the loss that weaves in and out of so many of her poems, the spirituality that brings in the earth and sea (she never moved far from the sea, her family bringing it with them from Sicily to New York and Long Island). As she sums up her life and her identity, perhaps the most fitting lines are these: "If there's music/ I dance/ if there's bingo/ I flee" (64).

LIFE SPAN DEVELOPMENT AND PARAMETERS OF CULTURE AND ACCULTURATION

These poems exude a sense of generativity in the naming and connecting up of generations within the poetry, as well as the passing of experiences, histories, culture, stories, customs, and traditions to the next generation and to the readers. While the very act of writing and creating poetry may in itself be seen as generative, this poetry's content also speaks to others in a way to share the writer's hard-earned wisdom, observations, and perspectives. Erikson (1963) felt that generativity was central to adult development, and, through this poetry, one can imagine the identity consolidation and further refinement that can occur in adulthood. The tension around Ego Integrity versus Despair clearly favors ego integrity in these poems, even if some hints of despair weave through now and then. The despair, though, is actually more of a longing and a sense of loss rather than despair that rails against fate or hides in a corner, defeated. Geluso is tackling the big and sometimes messy task of remembering, perhaps reliving, and recreating her life and her experience, and in the end seems to see it almost as an observer, acknowledging and affirming it for what it is and has been. For a woman in her eighties, these are some of the central issues of reworking a sense of self and identity — what can I give to those who come after me, and how has my life been? Yet there is another one of Erikson's stages that feels germane here, and some have argued it is a central one for women [see, e.g., Gilligan (1993)], that of Intimacy versus Isolation. For in so many of her poems, the quality and importance of relationships stand out, almost as if she is revisiting this theme, not really to rework it, but perhaps to affirm that her life has been one of intimacy with others.

Patterns of culture and acculturation are central to many of Geluso's poems, and, arguably, to the poet's sense of self and identity. Her family story of emigration, immigration, and acculturation took place in a particular context, which is felt throughout much of her work. How does one shed the old world yet not lose it? How does one take on the new world, yet keep the old values in one's heart? How do the important aspects of life, as one knew it, get redefined in a new land and a new time? How does one relate to the new authorities and the ever-changing customs in this new world? We see the love for family and for the old country and the strong desire to pass that on to the world and future generations of family; but this is a family also firmly rooted in the present time and space, just as the poetry is. The loss is palpable but not overwhelming.

ISSUES OF IDENTITY IN ITALIAN AMERICAN WOMEN

In this section, we ask questions about, and make suggestions for, working with Italian American women as clients in psychotherapy (individual, family, couple, or group) or in assessment, or as students or supervisees, based on what we have learned from the study of Italian American women poets. What are some of the sorrows, difficulties, or tensions for Italian American women in their creation of an identity and sense of self? What are important issues that need to be worked out or worked through? What are some of the strengths and resources of Italian American women and their capacity for identity development?

The story of emigration and immigration is the story of loss and discovery, separating and coming together, losing something and finding something. Thus, the poetry of Italian American women reflects the questions and experience of loss and discovery. How much can a person lose and still have something of value? How often can someone come back from a loss? What about those aspects of culture, family, and experience that one would want to lose, to close the door and walk away; yet they hold on, sometimes relentlessly? Perhaps the greatest loss is what can be called the Mother, which encompasses so much, such as the mother herself, nurturance, holding, the mother country—all that has been remembered as warm and life-giving from the old life. Along with loss, we see the resilience of moving forward, finding or creating something new and valuable, reconnecting or reworking old ties to home, family, lover, land, and, ultimately, to self. Is there a balance, a ratio, a way to measure the losses a person endures and the resilience she needs?

Given our framework of loss and resilience, the following suggestions may be helpful:

1. Identity is not just handed down to anyone, particularly those generations in transition, and transition may last a lot longer than one imagines. Identity must be actively constructed through living, reflecting, trying out new parts of oneself, taking appropriate risks, and coming back, enhanced, to one's sense of who one is.

2. Italian American women need to be supported to actively question the stereotypes, many of them destructive or at least limited, that the media present and that many women may swallow unthinkingly.

3. Knowing from where and whom you come is very important for some women, less obviously so for others, but is almost always lurking in the background regarding questions of identity.

4. For some women, losing a home, a land, or a community, such as a town or family in Italy, and actually finding it again, through travel or letters or reading, is important for them to be able to cultivate a sense of who they are and how that extends across time and place.

5. Connection and relationships have become almost clichés in thinking about Italian culture and about women. Yet, the complexity of connectedness is not a cliché. Rather, it forms the basis of the self from a very early point in life and continues throughout, even if connections are severed or have dwindled. Connectedness and attachment are not always positive, and are not always well understood, but loom large in Italian American culture and psyche. Giordano, McGoldrick, and Guarino Klages (2005) wrote of the complexity and centrality of family and extended family and friends for Italians, throughout the life cycle and in psychotherapy, and their perspective is definitely worth reviewing for anyone working with Italian American women and identity.

6. Given the importance of relationships, and the prevalence of loss, there is a great need for mourning and integration of the losses, or one risks becoming hollow or a caricature. That seems to be the basis for at least some of the stereotypes that develop. Ste-

reotypes grow from what is left and then magnified of unintegrated, unmetabolized issues of identity.

7. The poets represent possible stages of mourning for women to consider, such as absence or loss (which could be of a person, part of the self, one's culture, etc.) and idealization of what is lost, then acknowledgement of absence, which is followed by anger and hunger for the loss, and, finally, sadness and searching to create something new from that loss.

8. Looking over one's life and the current context, as one does in psychotherapy and also in poetry, can be very helpful in sorting out all of this and coming to some sense of perspective about who one is and how one lives in or makes changes in the current culture, whatever it may be. We suggest the reading of Italian American women's poetry, or encouraging women to write their own poetry, as an adjunct to psychotherapy for those clients who might be so inclined, as the poetry is very accessible and can bring up questions and solutions not considered.

9. If Italian American women do not define who they are, someone else (the latest bad television show, one's husband or father, one's friends, glaringly awful commercials, etc.) will do it for them, much to everyone's detriment and disfiguring.

10. When Italian Americans do take a stand and define who they are, as in the poetry considered here, we see acts of love, defiance, joy, sorrow, humor, defense, intelligence, strength, and struggle. In short, we see real human beings.

References

Alba, Richard. 2000. "The Twilight of Ethnicity among Americans of European Ancestry: The Case of the Italians." *The Review of Italian American Studies*, edited by Frank M. Sorrentino and Jerome Krase, 41–74. Lanham, MD: Lexington Books.

Albright, Carol B., and Christine P. Moore. 2011. *American Women, Italian Style: Italian Americana's Best Writings on Women*. New York: Fordham University Press.

Arredondo, Patricia, Rebecca Toporek, Sherlon P. Brown, Janet Sanchez, Don C. Locke, Joe Sanchez, and Holly Stadler. 1996. "Operationalization of the Multicultural Counseling Competencies." *Journal of Multicultural Counseling and Development* 24:42–78.

Barolini, Helen. 1985. *The Dream Book*. New York: Schocken Books.

Barreca, Regina. 2002. "Preface: Special Issue on Italian American literature." *LIT: Literature Interpretation Theory* 13(3):167–171.

Bayor, Ronald H. 2009. "Another Look at 'Whiteness': The Persistence of Ethnicity in American Life." *Journal of American Ethnic History* 29(1):13–30.

Eisenger, Amy. 2011. "Another Day at the 'Jersey Shore'; MTV Staff Receives Threats, Advertisers Bolt." *New York Daily News*. Retrieved March 18 from nydailynews.com.

Erikson, Erik H. 1963. *Childhood and Society*. New York: W. W. Norton.

_____, and Joan M. Erikson. 1997. *The Life Cycle Complete*. New York: W. W. Norton.

Falicov, Celia J. 1995. "Training to Think Culturally: A Multidimensional Comparative Framework." *Family Process*, 34, 373-388.

Gambino, Richard. 1997. "The Crisis of Italian American Identity." In *Beyond the Godfather: Italian American Writers on the Real Italian American Experience*, edited by A. Kenneth Ciongoli and Jay Parini, 269–288. Hanover, NH: University Press of New England.

Geluso, Josephine E. 2003. *Memories Served Here*. Bellmore, NY: Sheron Enterprises.

_____. 2005. *Flowering in December*. Stamford, NY: Stonecrest.

_____. 2007. *If There's Music I Dance*. Stamford, NY: Stonecrest.

Gilligan, Carol. 1993. *In a Different Voice: Psychological Theory and Women's Development*. Cambridge, MA: Harvard University Press.

Giordano, Joe, Monica McGoldrick, and Joanne Guarino Klages 2005. "Italian Families." In *Ethnicity and Family Therapy*, 3rd ed., edited by Monica McGoldrick, Joe Giordano, and Nydia Garcia-Preto, 616–628, New York: The Guilford Press.

Green, Andre. 2001. (A.Weller, Trans.). *Life Narcissism Death Narcissism*. London: Free Association Books. (original work published 1980).

Luconi, Stefano. 2004. "Becoming Italian in the US: Through the Lens of Life Narratives." *MELUS* 29(3/4):151–164.

McWilliams, Nancy.1999. *Psychoanalytic Case Formulation*. New York: Guilford Press.

Messina, Elizabeth. 1994. "Life-span development and Italian American Women." In *Italian Americans in a Multicultural Society* edited by Jerome Krase and Judith N. DeSena, 74-87. Stony Brook, NY: Forum Italicum.

Phinney, Jean S. 1996. "When We Talk about American Ethnic Groups, What Do We Mean?" *American Psychologist* 51:918–927.

Ryan, Sylvia F. 2008. "The Light of Fallen Stars." Retrieved March 30, 2011: http://italian americana.com/books/s.f.ryan.pdf

Vecoli, Rudolph J. 2000. "Are Italian Americans Just White Folks?" In *The Review of Italian American Studies*, edited by Frank M. Sorrentino and Jerome Krase, 75–88. Lanham, MD: Lexington Books.

Winnicott, Donald.W. 1971. *Playing and Reality*. London: Tavistock Publications.

Intimate Partner Violence Within the Italian American Community

ANTHONY F. TASSO
DANA KASPEREEN-GUIDICIPIETRO
JENNIFER L. TURSI

INTRODUCTION

Domestic violence (DV) or intimate partner violence (IPV) is broadly defined as relational abuse between people within close, intimate relationships. Encompassing physical, emotional, and verbal forms of abuse, the Centers for Disease Control and Prevention (CDC 2011) reported that partner-violent assaults amount to an estimated 7.7 million yearly acts (Tjaden and Thoennes 2000). Domestic violent homicides number more than 1500 annually (Department of Justice 2009), and the cumulative yearly financial impact of IPV (e.g., medical bills, loss of work) surpasses $8 billion (CDC 2003; Max et al. 2004). More disconcerting is that these statistics represent just what we know. DV is grossly underreported, with many mysterious injuries, illnesses, and psychological conditions never directly tied to relational abuse. In other words, the short-term and long-term DV sequelae regularly seen by those in the everyday practice of mental health treatment, social work, and protective services are likely just the small tip of a very large iceberg.

This essay explores the multilayered phenomenon of DV within the Italian American community. First, we provide a succinct descriptive overview of IPV. Second, we describe general Italian and Italian American cultural themes, followed by a more substantial and detailed examination of how specific Italian American cultural factors are likely to interact with intrapsychic/psychological phenomena relevant to DV. We conclude by exploring overall IPV treatment issues and the ways in which culturally competent clinicians can tailor interventions to most effectively address DV among Italian Americans.

DOMESTIC VIOLENCE THEORIES

Intimate partner violence is a destructive staple of human behavior knowing no religious, cultural, sexual orientation, or economic parameters. Although violence against a spouse or dating partner has always been a part of human relationships, the study of relational violence has historically been peripheral to mainstream psychology and psychological science due to an apparent lack of interest from major professional mental health organizations, to ideological squabbles, and to the secretiveness of family violence, among other reasons. The collective professional silence on DV has inadvertently resulted in the intensification, continuation, and perpetuation of IPV. It also means that the development of DV as a bona fide field of study has fallen outside the domain of scientific psychology or clinical practice.

With the mental health field all but ignoring the scientific examination of relational violence, the emergence of the DV field belongs to the feminist movement. Born out of the shelter movement of protecting abused women, feminist theory highlights the long-term societal, cultural, political, and religious messages that implicitly and explicitly endorse violence against women. Prominent feminist scholars such as Dobash and Dobash (1979) underscore the vast injustices aimed at women and argue how such processes facilitate and sustain violence against women.

Feminist, gender-based/sociopolitical views on DV etiology and intervention have been the dominant viewpoint. Sociopolitical explanations for DV posit that men use violence toward women as a means of maintaining their patriarchal dominance and subjugation (Bancroft 2002; Pence and McDonnell 2000; Saunders 2000). Abusive males are characterized by power and control, intimidation, economic manipulation, degradation, possessiveness, and sexual coercion. Feminist theory contends that traditional male socialization leads men and boys to restrict their emotional expressions only to anger, which often leads to violence — something that puts women and girls directly in harm's way.

The negation of the possibility of psychological or biologically based violence determinants is a key characteristic of feminist DV theory. In fact, sociopolitical approaches tenaciously hold to the idea that the root cause of DV is societal messages sanctioning violence against women, not psychopathology. Gender-based proponents often categorically oppose psychological perspectives of IPV due to the putative belief that such explanations exonerate the DV perpetrator (e.g., he has issues) in concert with pathologizing the victim (e.g., she's provocative). Feminist interventions instead are educational in nature, with the goal of challenging abusive men on their presumed sense of male entitlement and promoting the merits of egalitarianism (Pence and Paymar 1993).

Feminist advocates' accomplishments in addressing DV are prodigious, which include, but are not limited to, illuminating societal gender inequalities, exposing the pervasiveness of spousal abuse in the home, and initiating legal and community-based responses to violence against women (e.g., mandatory arrests, court-ordered IPV counseling)—none of which existed prior to the women's movement. Despite such achievements, there are significant limitations to gender-based etiologic and interventional views [see Dutton (2006, 2007) and Rosenbaum and Leisring (2003)]. For example, feminist theory struggles (if not fails) to differentiate the causal determinants between abusive and nonabusive men. It also is unable to account for homosexual DV, with prevalence rates often exceeding heterosexual IPV (Tjaden and Thoennes 2000), or partner-violent women, which also accounts for a sizable portion of DV (Archer 2000, 2002). Put another way, feminism has aided and continues to aid in protecting abused women but remains highly limited in its etiologic and conceptual contributions.

Psychologically grounded IPV conceptualizations firmly enlist both clinical experience and psychological science to identify underlying DV factors. Social learning theory indicates that children exposed to DV are disproportionately more likely to be involved in domestically violent relationships as adults compared to those not exposed to childhood family violence (Delsol and Margolin 2004; Ehrensaft et al. 2003; Godbout et al. 2009; Ireland and Smith 2009). However, some investigators have pointed out that the increased etiologic variance from childhood DV exposure is minimal [see Ehrensaft (2009)]. Nonetheless, such a psychological approach expands our understanding of experiences that predict IPV and helps explain different cognitive distortions (arbitrary inferences, overgeneralization, and magnification) and faulty beliefs about self and others common to relationally violent persons (Eckhardt and Kassinove 1998).

Psychoanalytic theory and developmental science offer even greater IPV etiological and conceptual power. Dutton (2006, 2007) and Nicolson (2010) called on the theoretical value of Margaret Mahler (Mahler, Pine, and Bergman 1975), Melanie Klein (Klein and Riviere 1937, 1964), and Donald Winnicott (1969) to explore further the underpinnings of DV.

Specifically, they described how rage reactions following perceived abandonment, splitting of a dating partner (e.g., "Madonna-whore" complex), a propensity to both worship and devalue a partner, fears of annihilation, and unneutralized "temper tantrums" explained by these theorists are pertinent to the relationally abusive person. [Splitting is defined as a mental mechanism in which the self or others are reviewed as all good or all bad, with failure to integrate the positive and negative qualities of self and others into cohesive images. Often the person alternately idealizes and devalues the same person (Abess 2012).]

These contemporary DV scholars utilize tried-and-true psychoanalytic theories and concepts to highlight the role of early developmental antecedents in parsing possible IPV casual factors as well as to elucidate key behavioral and intrapsychic experiences of domestically violent perpetrators.

Psychoanalytic explanations segue nicely to the role of attachment theory within IPV. Developed by John Bowlby (1969, 1973, 1980) and Maryann Ainsworth (Ainsworth et al. 1978), attachment theory offers significant insights into IPV. The psychobiological concept of attachment is based on the notion that infants are dependent on (or attached to) their parents or caregivers, and that this connection to a more powerful other is necessary for survival. This protracted infantile dependency promotes the need for the infant to unite with more physically and emotionally stable humans. In other words, infants and children have a healthy need to connect with their more powerful adult caregivers. When these affectional and physical needs are consistently met, the child develops a secure attachment, resulting in the internalization of the "goodness" and "protectiveness" of the parent(s). A healthy result is that securely attached children are able to be soothed following separations from caregivers. However, those children who do not have consistent, enduring parent(s) or parental-like figures develop what is collectively classified as insecure attachment styles. Insecurely attached children—and subsequently insecurely attached adults—develop a fundamental sense of anxiety, fear of abandonment, an inability to experience an emotionally evocative memory of significant others, and vexation during periods of separation.

How does attachment theory relate to DV? Theory, research, and clinical practice have identified the salience of insecure attachment styles in DV perpetrators and victims (Dutton 2007; Dutton et al. 1994; Mahalik et al. 2005; Mauricio and Gormley 2001; Tasso 2011; Tasso et al. 2010; Tasso et al. 2012). Attachment helps explain perpetrators' hypersensitivity to interpersonal slights, abandonment fears, and smothering jealously (Dutton 1995; Dutton, van Ginkel, and Starzomski 1995; Stosny 1995; Tasso 2012; Wexler 2006). Insecure attachments help explain IPV victims' enduring connectedness to and willingness to remain with abusive partners (Nicolson 2010; Young and Gerson 1991), as well as how early tumultuous attachment relationships obscure the ability to see adult relationships as destructive and personally dangerous (Blizard and Bluhm 1994; Brown and Kaspereen-Guidicipietro 2011).

ITALIAN/ITALIAN AMERICANS AND DOMESTIC VIOLENCE

The aforementioned concepts are relevant to DV in general [for a more exhaustive review, see O'Leary and Woodin (2009) and White, Koss, and Kazin (2011)]. However, what about cultural factors? Specifically, what about Italian American characteristics connected to IPV?

Although all major mental health associations (e.g., American Psychological Association, American Counseling Association, National Association of Social Work) emphasize the necessity for practicing clinicians to be mindful of culturally based factors relevant to the people they treat, there is a paucity of literature addressing patient work with Italian Americans and even less investigating Italian American DV. Although the mental health literature examining different ethnic and cultural groups is fast growing, professional attention to Italian American cultural research and clinical analysis is conspicuously lagging. Therefore, we first explore Italian American family structure and familial patterns followed by how these phenomena are potentially linked to IPV among Italian Americans.

One needs to look no further than pop culture and our daily vernacular to tap into what American society thinks of Italian American domestic relationships. Stereotypes would suggest that IPV runs rampant within the Italian American community. American men of Italian descent are depicted as highly controlling, demeaning, and abusive to women, while Italian American women are seen as reflexively servile to and victimized by their partners. Sleeveless, tank-top undershirts are often referred to as "Italian wife-beaters." Movies and television portray Italian American men proudly displaying mistresses (goumadas) of whom wives are often cognizant. (Goumada, derived from comare, which literally means "godmother," is the southern Italian slang for mistress.) These images imply the normalcy of such spousal boundary transgressions and suggest long-standing relational imbalances within Italian American couples.

Family and the preservation of the family unit are of paramount importance to Italian Americans (Giordano, McGoldrick, and Guarino Klages 2005; McAuliffe and Associates 2008). Italian and Italian American children are reared with an explicit understanding that family is sacrosanct. Italian Americans often remain a part of their nuclear families long beyond the standard Western college-aged timeframe. Italian Americans maintain an enduring connectedness to their parents and siblings even as adults with their own newly formed families. The family focus ethos of Italian culture often supersedes educational strivings, with children maintaining family-of-origin ties that are sometimes at the cost of higher educational pursuits (McCloskey et al. 2002).

The Italian American marital dyad warrants attention in exploring potentially relevant culture-specific factors linked to relational violence. Italian/Italian American intimate relationships typically adhere to more traditional gender roles and lean toward patriarchy (McAuliffe and Associates 2008). Although Italian American marriages and dating relationships are far from uniform, such domestic relationships tend to be male centered, with men assuming a more dominant relational and familial position, and women taking a more passive or secondary role. Fathers are seen as providers and protectors, while mothers are seen as the nurturers and the heart of the family's emotional support.

Masculinity, inextricably linked to DV, is also central to understanding Italian and Italian American culture. Tagar and Good (2005) empirically revealed that Italian males living in Italy present as outgoing, fearless, and restrictive of personal emotional expressiveness. They also believe women to be subservient to men. Although this investigation did not examine any links between these findings on Italian masculinity and DV with Italians and Italian Americans, Moore and Stuart (2005) summarized empirical evidence not specific to Italian culture, which indicated that perceived pressure not to veer from masculine socialization is predictive of IPV. Therefore, Tagar and Good's (2005) study provides promising etiologic data in conjunction with a powerful springboard for much needed Italian American IPV research.

Yaccarino (1993) suggested that Italian and Italian American femininity is defined as being a constant nurturer and supporter of the family's emotional needs. Both as mothers and young girls, people of Italian descent learn early through direct observation and verbalization from their venerable elders that to be a good Italian girl or woman means being a good nurturer. Food, which serves as a primary nurturing vehicle, takes on substantial significance for both holiday events and everyday gatherings. Yaccarino (1993) further reported that Italian American women are also tagged with the task of teaching children about their heritage and are, in essence, the overseers in assuring progeny are thoroughly informed of their familial and cultural norms. What does this mean? It underscores children's intense closeness with the mother and imbues her with the power of the emotional provider and guardian of the familial linage.

Italian Americans represent a large portion of practicing Catholics within the United States [see Blumberg and Lavin (2011)]. Palmisano (2010), however, reported on the growing trend of Italians and Italian Americans turning toward non-religion-based spirituality rather than traditional Catholic belief systems and describing themselves as spiritual but not religious. Although many DV scholars have argued that traditional religious affiliations can be detrimental to violence against women due to patriarchal messages, Ellison and Anderson (2001) revealed that men and women across religious denominations report lower rates of IPV among those who actively attend religious services than those who do not.

How does the family emphasis among Italians/Italian Americans factor into Italian American domestic violence?

McCloskey et al. (2002) indicated that Italian women in Italy report greater DV victimization than Italian women living in the United States, while Romito, Crisma, and Saurel-Cubizolles (2003) revealed that Italian women living in Italy who were abused by their parents as children were more likely to be involved in domestically violent relationships as adults than Italian women who were not abused as children. Such findings intimate that women both heavily immersed in Italian cultural norms and directly abused as children are more likely to be DV victims in adulthood. Therefore, the confluence of traditional Italian culture and the experience of family violence partially accounts for the intergenerational transmission of family violence with Italian women.

The close family unit common to the Italian culture creates potentially powerful challenges in addressing and treating DV (see the discussion about treatment options below). The literature underscores the sanctity of the Italian/Italian American family and emphasizes how Italian Americans will often vociferously work to protect the family name (Giordano et al. 2005; McCloskey et al. 2002). Although this can be a positive force in proactively protecting the family, when DV is present, this familial theme becomes counterproductive and poses a serious threat to addressing IPV on several levels. First, Italian American DV victims are often reluctant to seek help due to the necessity to expose familial secrets and, therefore, bring shame to the family. Additionally, DV perpetrators commonly resist reaching out for help due to an oft-crippling sense of shame [see Wallace and Nosko (2002)]. Also, such admission of familial abuse by Italian Americans inherently exacerbates shame due to a sense of failing to live up to cultural ideals of familial protectiveness and husbandry. In other words, Italian Americans' adherence to the adage of "what happens in the family, stays in the family" potentially fuels IPV and prevents victims and perpetrators from seeking much needed treatment.

In exploring the psychodynamics of childhood aggressive behaviors, Twemlow (2000) postulated that interpersonal hostility emerges due to: (a) Unconscious rage because of the need to forego merger fantasies with the mother; (b) unconscious fear of being unable to separate proactively from the mother's profound and pervasive influence; and (c) revenge fantasies symbolically aimed at motherlike figures due to the mother's perceived omnipotence and subsequent abandoning of her role as a personal guardian. Put otherwise, the child's presumed heightened intimacy with the mother conversely begets unconscious rage, fear, and the vengeful desire to destroy his early protector. Although Twemlow's (2000) work centered on the antecedents of school-age bullying, such processes appear to account nicely for not only IPV at large but also Italian American DV perpetration in particular. Specifically, the prominence of the mothering role in the child's emotional world and the tight connection between Italian American children (especially boys) and their mothers, coupled with boys often wearing their momma's boy status as a badge of honor, proves to be a recipe for intense passive-regressive yearnings. This conflictual experience of consciously celebrating such parental closeness, combined with the unconscious disdain for such longings for the more powerful mother, is fertile ground for anger and rage directed toward current intimate partners.

INTIMATE PARTNER VIOLENCE INTERVENTIONAL APPROACHES

What are the major interventional approaches for IPV perpetrators and victims? Furthermore, what are the most effective ways to intervene in DV with Italian Americans?

To address DV most effectively, clinicians, advocates, and concerned citizens should be mindful of the history, controversies, and extant research on IPV treatment. The first and most popular approach to IPV intervention is the feminist approach. Based on the premise that the genesis of DV is gender role socialization (not psychopathology), feminist DV perpetration interventions are psychoeducative, challenging men on their sexist attitudes, male entitlement, dominance, and control over women. Pence and Paymar's (1993) feminist approach to IPV perpetration remains the most widely used of any intervention. It is important to note that despite the preeminence of gender-based interventions, the investigations on the effectiveness of profeminist educational approaches for partner-violent men fail to garner empirical support [see Babcock, Green, and Robie (2004) and Bowen, Gilchrist, and Beech (2005)].

Feminist IPV victim services aim to educate victims about society's dismissive view of women and its belief that violence toward women is acceptable. Empowerment counseling is also fundamental, with the goal of providing battered women the inner strength that was likely lost as a result of the abuse. Feminist approaches avoid any implication of psychologically based factors that facilitate relational abuse or victimization. Instead, the foci center on empowerment, social messages, and support. Such approaches for DV victims are the prevailing support methods offered in battered women's shelters. Although these collective interventions have only been minimally open to scientific examination, Sullivan (2011) indicated that there is some empirical support for these victim services.

Maiuro and Eberle (2008) reported on the growing paradigm shift in the federal standards for DV perpetration treatment, which now firmly enlist psychologically informed treatments. Leaning on a growing body of evidence suggesting the need to address DV psychotherapeutically (rather than just educationally), the approach is now using traditional theoretical clinical approaches and modalities to treat DV perpetrators (e.g., Cogan and Porcerelli 2002; Morrel et al. 2003; Musser et al. 2008) as well as victims (Feske 2008; Mulick, Landes, and Kanter 2005; Resick et al. 2008; Turnage, Jacinto, and Kirven 2003). A group treatment approach remains the most widely used modality with perpetrators (Rosenbaum and Kunkel 2009) and victims (Mendelsohn, Zachary, and Harney 2007). Group treatment for perpetrators allows for between-member accountability, as well as for the reduction of shame via IPV perpetrators sharing their experiences of spousal assault (Wallace and Nosko 2002). For victims, group treatment facilitates a sense of closeness and belonging, which helps counter the intense isolation that often accompanies DV victimization.

Individual psychotherapy is also used in IPV perpetrator and victim treatment, either as the lone interventional approach or in conjunction with group treatment (Murphy, Meis, and Eckhardt 2009). Individual psychotherapy enables the clinician to tailor interventions that best meet persons' needs, such as specific attention to comorbid conditions (e.g., substance abuse, psychiatric symptomatologies, family-of-origin themes), and provides the patient with greater comfort in discussing emotionally difficult experiences, abuse related or otherwise. Evidence suggests the combination of group and individual treatment is the best approach for domestically violent perpetrators (Cogan and Porcerelli 2002).

TREATMENT IMPLICATIONS FOR ITALIAN AMERICANS

How do psychotherapeutic IPV approaches best help in the treatment of DV with Italian Americans? First, scientific and clinical data indicate the heterogeneity of domestically violent relationships (Johnson 1995, 2008). Similarly, Italian Americans are a diverse group, with great variability in generational factors, religious affiliations, and perceived identification with cultural heritage.

The extent of identification with Italian heritage helps determine treatment pacing and possible treatment barriers. For example, Italian Americans have historically undervalued college aspirations due to the ostensible belief that such a pursuit would not provide immediate help for the family (Giordano et al. 2005). Given that college-educated people are more likely to voluntarily access mental health services than non-college-educated people, the lack of education among many Italian Americans unfortunately leads to the underutilization of talk therapy. Although the Calandra Institute (2000) optimistically suggests that more Italian Americans are seeing the practicality of higher education (thus, offering the hope of greater willingness to seek psychotherapeutic services), one can assume Italian Americans currently use psychotherapy less than other cultural groups.

There is a commonly held Italian/Italian American value that dialogue about private family issues, even with a professional, is anathema. Giordano et al. (2005) suggest that because of this cultural value of keeping family matters private, an Italian American seeking treatment will possibly be in crisis. Therapists are thus confronted with both the reluctance to discuss family matters (especially family violence) and the probability that the clients/patients are in the midst of intrapersonal and/or interpersonal calamities.

Given the family emphasis, an early therapeutic task with Italian Americans involved in DV is to explicitly establish safe treatment parameters. Addressing professional boundaries (e.g., confidentiality, duty to warn), which is difficult enough when dealing with IPV because of the ever-present concerns of imminent danger, is even more challenging with Americans of Italian descent. Culturally sensitive practitioners need to convincingly convey to Italian American patients that revealing personal and familial experiences does not contradict their core family values, but rather that openly discussing problems can enhance the inherent strength of the family. In addition, clinicians need to balance investigating destructive familial aspects with affirming the person's family values, strengths, and protectiveness. This underscores the clinical task of creating a safe, permissive, therapeutic environment in which an Italian American patient feels comfortable exploring such familial dynamics.

Such techniques are no easy task, especially with Italian American DV. If clinicians focus too narrowly on possible family strengths, or worse, if they iatrogenically create such strengths that are nonexistent, they inadvertently collude with individual and familial pathology as well as fail to connect empathically with the individual. This renders treatment ineffective and DV persists. In other words, counselors tasked with addressing IPV with Italian American individuals need to carefully balance reinforcing preexisting strengths about self and others (especially those relating to family) with inquiring delicately about family violence in order for treatment to have the potential to be successful.

Clinical work with Italian American partner-violent men regularly illuminates the early mother–child experience (e.g., Twemlow 2000) vis-à-vis current domestically violent relationships. Relationally abusive Italian American men frequently present with complaints that their spouse or dating partner fails to meet their practical and emotional needs. Upon further inquiry, such men strikingly and openly verbalize how their partners' efforts fall short of the high standards set forth by their mothers. During treatment, men of Italian decent often reveal the unrealistic demands placed on their romantic partners, probably born out of their infantilized neediness and unconscious remembrance of the early mother–

child unit. However, full awareness of such primitive desires causes anxiety; therefore, when such passive-regressive fantasies threaten to become conscious, the domestically violent man resorts to attacking the very person he currently needs. Now it is she who is fearful, not he. This process converts his passivity into transient omnipotence. He no longer needs his spouse or dating partner, but rather dominates her, the person who currently provides his dependency needs, and who is emblematic of his most primal nurturer (i.e., mother). This is a prominent theme with domestically violent Italian American men, irrespective of the cultural background of romantic partners.

Italian Americans, especially those who adhere to more traditional cultural values, often resist divorce (McCloskey et al. 2002). Although divorce is not a requisite for adequately addressing domestically violent relationships, the topic is inherently present in IPV treatment, especially with victims whose partners appear unyielding in their abusiveness. Whether this reluctance to consider divorce is rooted in Catholicism, family preservation, or both, psychotherapists need to be aware that for Italians Americans (and others) the decision to terminate a marriage is complex. In addition to cultural and religious factors, there are financial concerns, as well as psychologically based determinants, that unconsciously connect persons to destructive others (e.g., re-creation of early family dynamics). Therefore, clinicians need to be careful not to imply overtly or covertly that divorce is necessary. At the same time, therapists must be cognizant of their verbal and nonverbal reactions that suggest disapproval of a patient's desire to remain with a presumed unhealthy partner.

Traditional boilerplate IPV protocols (e.g., gender-based interventions) are designed to treat persons nomothetically, ultimately missing the idiographic aspects of those being treated. In contrast, psychologically and culturally grounded treatments adhere to the notion that we treat people, not a collection of behaviors. Therefore, sophisticated psychotherapeutic treatments provide the greatest flexibility to address cultural and psychological factors germane to Italian Americans, concurrently. Such approaches allow astute therapists to address personality factors and familial dynamics—all of which allow for greater access to psychological and psychocultural themes necessary to treat Italian Americans in the throes of IPV.

Skilled IPV clinical practitioners working with Italian Americans need to be mindful of the delicacy in their approach with which they explore current marital dynamics. Inquiring about family-of-origin issues may require even greater caution. The intense familial closeness, the sensitivity to perceived slurs against the family, and the defensive, overdetermined need to protect the image of the family are often substantial difficulties in initiating treatment. Italian Americans will often experience discussions of their childhood as transgressing unspoken (though powerful) sociocultural boundaries. Although proactively confronting these resistances is crucial to the treatment process, pacing such interventions around patient/client readiness to engage in such emotionally exasperating discussions is also critical. Therefore, therapists need to establish a strong therapeutic alliance informed by solid psychological training and steeped in Italian American cultural awareness.

The above-mentioned themes are psychologically and ethnoculturally anchored treatment approaches to DV with Italian Americans that are available once IPV has occurred. However, what about preventative measures? How can professionals and concerned citizens prevent relational violence within Italian American communities? It would be remiss of us to neglect an opportunity to touch on those methods aimed at preventing DV or to omit exploring how preexisting programs apply to Italian Americans. Primary preventative measures' target audience is children and teenagers who have not yet commenced full-fledged dating relationships. Many teen programs exist [for review see Foshee, McNaughton Reyes, and Wyckoff (2009) and Teten et al. (2009)]. Dating violence prevention programs focus on educating youths about healthy dating, respect for self and others, and identifying harbingers of dating abuse. Foshee and colleagues (Foshee and McNaughton Reyes 2009; Foshee et al. 2009) stated that in addition to targeting children, preventative curricula also aim to educate parents on the signs of dating abuse. Murray, Tasso, and Hawkins-Rodgers (2011) reported that such processes consist of trained teachers, educators, or counselors conducting the programs (usually on school grounds) over the course of five to twenty four-hour-long sessions, while Staggs and Schewe (2011) stated that interactive preventative programs are the most effective. Although the deleterious aspects of dating need to be addressed within such programs, professionals must also emphasize the positive messages about dating relationships and avoid fear-based themes (Strauss 2009).

Addressing the perception of gender inequality and the presumed culture of violence is imperative in any prevention program targeting

Italian Americans. Giordano et al. (2005) reported that more than seventy percent of Americans believe that most Italian Americans are connected to the mafia. Concomitant is the belief that men of Italian descent value subservient women, while women of Italian descent value domineering men. Preventative measures need to illuminate how such beliefs about the acceptability of violence and gender power differentials are, at best, counterproductive to healthy relationships and, at worst, contributive to relational violence.

CONCLUSION

We are currently limited in our abilities to prevent and to intervene with identified DV incidents within the Italian American community. Current theory and research do not comprehensively account for IPV etiology. Extant IPV literature on Italians and Italian Americans is even sparser, with only a handful of theoretical and empirical studies specifically targeting relational violence themes among Italian Americans. This is a serious problem. Given the intricacies of DV within Italian American communities, a partnering of researchers, psychotherapists, and Italian American scholars is needed to shed light on the causes and treatment of Italian American couples and families mired in the devastation of IPV.

Domestically violent and/or domestically abused persons are a diverse group, as are Italian Americans. Therefore, Italian Americans involved in IPV require astute clinicians who are abreast of DV theory and research and are in tune with Italian American culture. Ignorance or naïveté in either domain leaves the Italian American IPV perpetrator perilously bereft of options, the Italian American family without the best chance to cease relational violence, and the Italian American victim in continued danger.

References

Abess, John F. 2012. "Terms in the Field of Psychiatry and Neurology." Accessed June 26: http://www.abess.com/glossary.html.

Ainsworth, Mary D. S., Mary C. Blehar, Everett Waters, and Sally Wall. 1978. *Patterns of Attachment: A Psychological Study of the Strange Situation*. Hillsdale, NJ: Erlbaum.

Archer, John. 2000. "Sex Differences in Aggression between Heterosexual Partners: A Meta-Analytic Review." *Psychological Bulletin* 126(5):651–680.

_____. 2002. "Sex Differences in Physically Aggressive Acts between Heterosexual Partners: A Meta-Analytic Review." *Aggression and Violent Behavior* 7(4):313–351.

Babcock, Julia C., Charles E. Green, and Chet Robie. 2004. "Does Batterers' Treatment Work? A Meta-Analytic Review of Domestic Violence Treatment." *Clinical Psychology Review* 23(8): 1023–1053.

Bancroft, Lundy. 2002. *Why Does He Do That? Inside the Minds of Angry and Controlling Men.* New York: Berkley Books.

Blizard, Ruth A., and Ann M. Bluhm. 1994. "Attachment to the Abuser: Integrating Object-Relations and Trauma Theories in Treatment of Abuse Survivors." *Psychotherapy* 31(3):383–390.

Blumberg, Audrey, and David E. Lavin. 2011. "Italian-American Students at the City University of New York: A Socioeconomic and Educational Profile." In *Italian-American Students in New York City, 1975–2000: A Research Anthology,* Vol. 3, edited by Nancy L. Ziehler, 113–135, New York: The John D. Calandra Italian American Institute.

Bowen, Erica, Elizabeth A. Gilchrist, and Anthony R. Beech. 2005. "An Examination of the Impact of Community-Based Rehabilitation on the Offending Behaviour of Male Domestic Violence Offenders and the Characteristics Associated with Recidivism." *Legal and Criminological Psychology* 10(2): 189–209.

Bowlby, John. 1969. *Attachment and Loss: Attachment.* New York: Penguin Books.

_____. 1973. *Attachment and Loss: Separation.* New York: Penguin Books.

_____. 1980. *Attachment and Loss: Loss, Sadness, and Depression.* New York: Penguin Books.

Brown, Donalee, and Dana Kaspereen-Guidicipietro. 2011. "Domestic Violence Victims." *New Jersey Psychologist* 61(2): 25–27.

Calandra Institute. 2000. *Educational Achievement Level of Italian-American Students in New York City Public Schools.* New York: Author.

Centers for Disease Control: National Center for Injury Prevention and Control. 2003. "Costs of Intimate Partner Violence Against Women in the United States." Atlanta, GA: Centers for Disease Control and Prevention (CDC).

_____. 2010. "Understanding Intimate Partner Violence: Fact Sheet 2011. Accessed September 21: http://www.cdc.gov/violenceprevention/pdf/IPV_factsheet-a.pdf.

Cogan, Rosemary, and John H. Porcerelli. 2002. "Psychoanalytic Psychotherapy with People in Abusive Relationships: Treatment Outcome." In *Intimate Violence: Contemporary Treatment Innovations,* edited by Donald Dutton and Daniel J. Sonkin, 29–46. New York: Haworth Press.

Delsol, Catherine, and Gayla Margolin. 2004. "The Role of Family-of-Origin Violence in Men's Marital Violence Perpetration." *Clinical Psychology Review* 24(1): 99–122.

Department of Justice, Bureau of Justice Statistics. 2009. "Homicide Trends in the United States." Accessed September 2: http://www.ojp.usdoj.gov/bjs/homicide/tables/intimatestab.htm.

Dobash, R. Emerson, and Russell P. Dobash. 1979. *Violence against Wives: A Case against the Patriarchy.* New York: Free Press.

Dutton, Donald G. 1995. *The Batterer: A Psychological Profile.* New York: Basic Books.

_____. 2006. *Rethinking Domestic Violence.* Canada: University of British Columbia Press.

_____. 2007. *Abusive Personality: Violence and Control in Intimate Relationships,* 2nd ed. New York: Guilford Press.

_____, Keith Saunders, Andrew Starzomski, and Kim Bartholomew. 1994. "Intimacy-Anger and Insecure Attachment as Precursors of Abuse in Intimate Relationships." *Journal of Applied Social Psychology* 24(15):1367–1386.

_____, Cynthia van Ginkel, and Andrew Starzomski. 1995. "The Role of Shame and Guilt in the Intergenerational Transmission of Abusiveness." *Violence and Victims* 10(2):121–131.

Ehrensaft, Miriam K. 2009. "Family and Relationship Predictors of Psychological and Physical Aggression." In *Psychological and Physical Aggression in Couples: Causes and Interventions,* edited by K. Daniel O'Leary and Erica M. Woodin, 99–118. Washington, DC: American Psychological Association.

_____, Patricia Cohen, Jocelyn Brown, Elizabeth Smailes, Henian Chen, and Jeffrey G. Johnson. 2003. "Intergenerational Transmission of Partner Violence: A 20-Year Prospective Study." *Journal of Consulting & Clinical Psychology* 71(4):741–753.

Eckhardt, Christopher I., and Howard Kassinove. 1998. "Articulated Cognitive Distortions and Cognitive Deficiencies in Maritally Violent Men." *Journal of Cognitive Psychotherapy* 12(3):231–250.

Ellison, Christopher G., and Kristin L. Anderson. 2001. "Religious Involvement and Domestic Violence among U.S. Couples." *Journal for the Scientific Study of Religion* 40(2):269–286.

Feske, Ulrike. 2008. "Treating Low-Income and Minority Women with Posttraumatic Stress Disorder: A Pilot Study Comparing Treatment as Usual Conducted by Community Therapists." *Journal of Interpersonal Violence* 23(8):1027–1040.

Foshee, Vangie A., and Heathe Luz McNaughton Reyes. 2009. "Primary Prevention of Adolescent Dating Abuse Perpetration: When to Begin, Whom to Target, and How to Do It." In *Preventing Partner Violence: Research and Evidence-Based Intervention Strategies,* edited by Daniel J. Whitaker and John R. Lutzker, 141–168. Washington, DC: American Psychological Association.

_____, Heathe Luz McNaughton Reyes, and Sarah C. Wyckoff. 2009. "Approaches to Preventing Psychological, Physical, and Sexual Partner Abuse." In *Psychological and Physical Aggression in Couples: Causes and Interventions,* edited by K. Daniel O'Leary and Erica M. Woodin, 165–189. Washington, DC: American Psychological Association.

Giordano, Joe, Monica McGoldrick, and Joanne Guarino Klages. 2005. "Italian Families." In *Ethnicity and Family Therapy,* 3rd ed., edited by Monica McGoldrick, Joe Giordano, and Nydia Garcia-Preto, 616–628. New York: Guildford Press.

Godbout, Natacha, Donald G. Dutton, Yvan Lussier, and Stephane Sabourin. 2009. "Early Exposure to Violence, Domestic Violence, Attachment Representations, and Marital Adjustment." *Personal Relationships* 16(3):365–384.

Ireland, Timothy O., and Carolyn A. Smith. 2009. "Living in Partner-Violent Families: Developmental Links to Antisocial Behavior and Relationship Violence." *Journal of Youth & Adolescence* 38(3):323–339.

Johnson, Michael P. 1995. "Patriarchal Terrorism and Common Couple Violence: Two Forms of Violence Against Women." *Journal of Marriage and the Family* 57(2):283–294.

_____. 2008. *A Typology of Domestic Violence: Intimate Terrorism, Violent Resistance, and Situational Couple Violence*. Boston: Northeastern University Press.

Klein, Melanie, and Joan Riviere. 1937. *Love, Hate and Reparation*. Norton: New York.

_____. 1964. *Love, Hate and Reparation,* 2nd ed. Norton: New York.

Mahalik, James R., Etiony Aldarondo, Steven Gilbert-Gokhale, and Erika Shore. 2005. "The Role of Insecure Attachment and Gender Role Stress in Predicting Controlling Behaviors in Men Who Batter." *Journal of Interpersonal Violence* 20(5):617–631.

Mahler, Margaret, Fred Pine, and Anni Bergman. 1975. *The Psychological Birth of the Human Infant.* New York: Basic Books.

Maiuro, Roland D., and Jane A. Eberle. 2008. "State Standards for Domestic Violence Perpetrator Treatment: Current Status, Trends, and Recommendations." *Violence & Victims* 23(2):133–155.

Mauricio, Anne Marie, and Barbara Gormley. 2001. "Male Perpetration of Physical Violence against Female Partners: The Interaction of Dominance Needs and Attachment Insecurity." *Journal of Interpersonal Violence* 16(10):1066–1081.

Max, Wendy, Dorothy P. Rice, Eric Finkelstein, Robert A. Bardwell, and Steven Leadbetter. 2004. "The Economic Toll of Intimate Partner Violence against Women in the United States." *Violence and Victims* 19(3):259–272.

McAuliffe, Garrett and Associates. 2008. *Culturally Alert Counseling: A Comprehensive Introduction.* Thousand Oaks, CA: Sage.

McCloskey, Laura Ann, Michaela Treviso, Theresa Scionti, and Giuliana dal Pozzo. 2002. "A Comparative Study of Battered Women and Their Children in Italy and the United States." *Journal of Family Violence* 17(1):53–74.

Mendelsohn, Michaela, Robin S. Zachary, and Patricia A. Harney. 2007. "Group Therapy as an Ecological Bridge to New Community for Trauma Survivors." *Journal of Aggression Maltreatment and Trauma* 14(1):227–243.

Moore, Todd M., and Gregory L. Stuart. 2005. "A Review of the Literature on Masculinity and Partner Violence." *Psychology of Men & Masculinity* 6(1):46–61.

Morrel, Tanya M., Jeffrey D. Elliott, Christopher M. Murphy, and Casey T. Taft. 2003. "Cognitive Behavioral and Supportive Group Treatments for Partner-Violent Men." *Behavioral Therapy* 34(1):77–95.

Mulick, Patrick S., Sara J. Landes, and Jonathan W. Kanter. 2005. "Contextual Behavior Therapies in the Treatment of PTSD: A Review." *International Journal of Behavioral Consultation and Therapy* 1(3):223–238.

Murphy, Christopher M., Laura A. Meis, and Christopher I. Eckhardt. 2009. "Individualized Services and Individual Therapy for Partner Abuse Perpetrators." In *Psychological and Physical Aggression in Couples: Causes and Interventions,* edited by K. Daniel O'Leary and Erica M. Woodin, 211–231. Washington, DC: American Psychological Association.

Murray, Morgan, Anthony F. Tasso, and Yolanda Hawkins-Rodgers. 2011. "Teen Dating Abuse." *New Jersey Psychologist* 61(3):28–31.

Musser, Peter H., Joshua N. Semiatin, Casey T. Taft, and Christopher M. Murphy. 2008. "Motivational Interviewing as Pregroup Intervention for Partner-Violent Men." *Violence & Victims* 23(5):539–557.

Nicolson, Paula. 2010. *Domestic Violence and Psychology: A Critical Perspective.* London: Routledge.

O'Leary, K. Daniel, and Erica M. Woodin. 2009. *Psychological and Physical Aggression in Couples: Causes and Interventions.* Washington, DC: American Psychological Association.

Palmisano, Stafania. 2010. "Spirituality and Catholicism: The Italian Experience." *Journal of Contemporary Religion* 25(2):221–241.

Pence, Ellen, and Michael Paymar. 1993. *Education Groups for Men Who Batter: The Duluth Model.* New York: Springer.

Pence, Ellen L., and Coral McDonnell. 2000. "Developing Policies and Protocols in Duluth, Minnesota." In *Home Truths about Domestic Violence: Feminist Influences on Policy and Practice – A Reader,* edited by Jalna Hammer and Catherine Itzin, 249–268. London: Routledge.

Resick, Patricia A., Tara E. Galovski, Mary O'Brien Uhlmansiek, Christine D. Scher, Gretchen A. Clum, and Yinong Young-Xu. 2008. "A Randomized Clinical Trial to Dismantle Components of Cognitive Processing Therapy for Posttraumatic Stress Disorder in Female Victims of Interpersonal Violence." *Journal of Counseling and Clinical Psychology* 76(2):243–258.

Romito, Patrizia, Michaela Crisma, and Marie-Josèphe Saurel-Cubizolles. 2003. "Adult Outcomes in Women Who Experienced Parental Violence During Childhood." *Child Abuse and Neglect* 27:1127–1144.

Rosenbaum, Alan, and Penny A. Leisring. 2003. "Beyond Power and Control: Towards an Understanding of Partner Abusive Men." *Journal of Comparative Family Studies* 34(1):7–22.

_____, and Tracii S. Kunkel. 2009. "Group Interventions for Intimate Partner Violence." In *Psychological and Physical Aggression in Couples: Causes and Interventions,* edited by K. Daniel O'Leary and Erica M. Woodin, 191–210. Washington, DC: American Psychological Association.

Saunders, Daniel G. 2000. "Feminist, Cognitive, and Behavioral Group Interventions for Men Who Batter: An Overview of Rationale and Methods." In *Domestic Violence 2000 Group Leader's Manual: An Integrated Skills Program for Men,* edited by David B. Wexler, 21-31. New York: Norton.

Staggs, Susan L., and Paul A. Schewe. 2011. "Primary Prevention of Domestic Violence." In *Violence against Women and Children: Navigating Solutions,* Vol. 2, edited by Mary P. Koss, Jacquelyn W. White, and Alan E. Kazdin, 237–257. Washington, DC: American Psychological Association.

Stosny, Steven. 1995. *Treating Attachment Abuse: A Compassionate Approach.* New York: Springer.

Strauss, Murray A. 2009. "Gender Symmetry in Partner Violence: Evidence and Implications for Prevention and Treatment." In *Preventing Partner Violence: Research and Evidence-Based Intervention Strategies,* edited by Daniel J. Whitaker and John R. Lutzker, 245–271. Washington, DC: American Psychological Association.

Sullivan, Chris M. 2011. "Victim Services for Domestic Violence." In *Violence against Women and Children: Navigating Solutions,* Vol. 2, edited by Mary P. Koss, Jacquelyn W. White, and Alan E. Kazdin, 183–197. Washington, DC: American Psychological Association.

Tagar, David, and Glenn E. Good. 2005. "Italian and American Masculinities: A Comparison of Masculine Gender Role Norms." *Psychology of Men & Masculinity* 6(4):264–274.

Tasso, Anthony. 2011. "Domestic Violence Perpetrators: Theory, Research, and Intervention." *New Jersey Psychologist* 61(2):20–24.

_____. 2012. "A Case Study of an Integrative Intervention with a Domestic Violence Perpetrator." *New Jersey Journal of Professional Counseling,* 61:2–13.

_____, Donalee Brown, Robert Griffo, and Ketrin Saud-Maxwell. 2012. "The Use of the Adult Attachment Scale with Domestically Violent Men." *The Journal of Family Violence* 27(8):731-739.

_____, Donalee Brown, Dana Kaspereen, Jennifer Tursi, Melanie Gibbons, and Robert Griffo. 2010. "Attachment Tendencies vis-à-vis Domestic Violence Perpetrators." Presented at the New Jersey Counseling Association annual conference, New Jersey.

Teten, Andra L., Barbara Ball, Linda Anne Valle, Rita Noonan, and Barr Rosenbluth. 2009. "Considerations for the Definition, Measurement, Consequences, and Prevention of Dating Violence Victimization Among Adolescent Girls." *Journal of Women's Health* 18(7):923–927.

Tjaden, Patricia, and Nancy Thoennes. 2000. "Prevalence, Incidence, and Consequences of Violence against Women: Findings from the National Violence against Women Survey." *U.S. Department of Justice. National Institute of Justice Centers for Disease Control and Prevention*: 2–18.

Turnage, Barbara F., George A. Jacinto, and Joshua Kirven. 2003. "Reality Therapy, Domestic Violence Survivors, and Self-Forgiveness." *International Journal of Reality Therapy* 22(2):23–27.

Twemlow, Stuart W. 2000. "The Roots of Violence: Converging Psychoanalytic Explanatory Models for Power Struggles and Violence in Schools." *Psychoanalytic Quarterly* 69:741–785.

Wallace, Robert, and Anna Nosko. 2002. "Shame in Male Spouse Abusers and Its Treatment in Group Therapy." In *Intimate Violence: Contemporary Treatment Innovations,* edited by Donald Dutton and Daniel J. Sonkin, 47–74. New York: Haworth Press.

Wexler, David B. 2006. *Stop Domestic Violence: Group Leaders Manual.* London: Norton & Company.

White, Jacquelyn W., Mary P. Koss, and Alan E. Kazdin. 2011. *Violence against Women and Children: Mapping the Terrain.* Washington, DC: American Psychological Association.

Winnicott, Donald W. 1969. "The Use of an Object." *International Journal of Psychoanalysis* 50:711–716.

Yaccarino, Elaine. 1993. "Using Minuchin's Structural Family Therapy Techniques with Italian-American Families." *Contemporary Family Therapy* 15(6):459–466.

Young, George H., and Samuel Gerson. 1991. "New Psychoanalytic Perspectives on Masochism and Spouse Abuse." *Psychotherapy* 28(1):30–38.

Contributors

Contributors

KATHRYN P. ALESSANDRIA, PHD, is Chair and an Associate Professor of Counselor Education at West Chester University. She is a first-generation Italian American and began studying ethnic identity in 1997. Her dissertation addressed ethnic identity salience for first-generation Italian Americans. Currently she is investigating postimmigration persistence of Italian American ethnic identity. Alessandria's interests also center on the role of college in developing ethnic identity. She has facilitated seminars for Italian American youth and was interviewed by RAI Television on the topic. Alessandria has written and presented extensively on the topics of ethnic identity and incorporating culture into counseling with white ethnic groups.

CHRISTINA BRUNI, MLS, earned a BA in English with honors from the College of Staten Island, CUNY. She obtained a masters degree in library and information Science from Pratt Institute, and has been a public service librarian with the Brooklyn Public Library for more than twelve years. Bruni is also the Health Guide for healthcentral.com/schizophrenia, a website hosted by HealthCentral, the third largest Internet health information provider. She does public speaking for the National Alliance on Mental Illness (NAMI), where she talks about her recovery.

DONNA M. CHIRICO, EDD, is Professor of Psychology and Chair of the Department of Behavioral Sciences at York College, CUNY. Her field research in India studying moral and spiritual development constitutes the foundation for her ongoing research program exploring the nature of imagination as it relates to aspects of psychological development. One implication is the role of the imaginative process in educational attainment among Americans of Italian descent. In a secondary project, Chirico looks at identity psychology as this relates to personal experience as an American of Italian descent. Matters of personal identity formation are being explored to achieve a better understanding of how ethnic identity contributes to psychological development of the self.

DONNA DICELLO, PSYD, is the Associate Director of the clinical psychology doctoral program at the University of Hartford. Her research interests include ethnicity and professional development, as well as grief and bereavement. DiCello has presented at conferences on grief work and Italian American mental health issues, and with her colleague, Dr. Lorraine Mangione, has a forthcoming book entitled *Daughters, Dads, and the Path of Grieving: Tales from Italian America* (Impact Publishing, Inc.). She was also lead author for a manuscript entitled "Contra Genio: The Experience of the Italian American Female Psychologist." DiCello also maintains a psychotherapy practice in New Haven, CT.

GIL FAGIANI, MSW, was a founder of the political organization White Lightning (1971-75). A social worker and addiction specialist, he directed Renewal House, a residential program for recovering alcoholics and drug addicts in downtown Brooklyn for twenty-one years. Fagiani is a founding member of The East Harlem Historical Organization, the Vito Marcantonio Forum, and a member of the Board of Directors of the Italian American Writers Association. A translator and writer, he has published six collections of his own poetry. His latest book, *Serfs of Psychiatry*, was inspired by the twelve years he worked at a state psychiatric hospital in the Bronx.

RICHARD GAMBINO, PhD, holds a doctorate in philosophy from New York University, and is Professor Emeritus at Queens College, CUNY, where, in 1973, he founded the first college-level Italian American Studies Program in the United States. He authored *Blood of My Blood: The Dilemma of Italian Americans* (1974). For seven semesters in the 1990s, he was a visiting professor at SUNY/Stony Brook, and started the Italian American Studies Program there. His 1977 book, *Vendetta*, a history of the largest lynching in United States of eleven Italian Americans in 1891, was made into a fictionalized feature film by HBO in 1999.

FRED GARDAPHÈ, PhD, is Distinguished Professor of English and Italian American Studies at Queens College, CUNY, and the John D. Calandra Italian American Institute, and he is the former director of Stony Brook University's American and Italian/American Studies programs. His books include *Italian Signs, American Streets: The Evolution of Italian American Narrative, Dagoes Read: Tradition and the Italian/American Writer, Moustache Pete is Dead!, Leaving Little Italy, From Wiseguys to Wise Men: Masculinities and the Italian American Gangster*, and *The Art of Reading Italian Americana: Italian American Culture in Review*. He is the cofounder and coeditor of *VIA: Voices in Italian Americana* and editor of the Italian American Culture Series of SUNY Press.

LUCIA IMBESI, MSW, is a psychoanalyst in private practice in New York City. She earned a master's degree in clinical psychology from Saint John's University and a master's degree in social work from Yeshiva University. She received her certificate in psychoanalysis from the Postgraduate Psychoanalytic Institute, where she served as a faculty member. She has also taught and supervised at Washington Square Institute, New York City. She has published several articles on various psychoanalytic topics, including: The etiology of narcissistic personality disorder; the role of the father in the development of masculinity; failures of insight in psychotherapy; and the impact of preverbal experience on defensive functions.

DANA KASPEREEN-GUIDICIPIETRO, PHD, earned an MA in Counseling and a PhD in Clinical Psychology. She is a Licensed Professional Counselor (LPC), a Licensed Clinical Alcohol & Drug Counselor (LCADC), a National Certified Counselor (NCC), an Approved Clinical Supervisor (ACS), a National Board Certified Clinical Hypnotherapist (NBCCH), and a Substance Abuse Coordinator (SAC). She is an Assistant Professor at Fairleigh Dickinson University in New Jersey, and has a private practice in Florham Park, NJ.

MARIA A. (OLA) KOPACZ, PHD, is an Assistant Professor in the Department of Communication Studies at West Chester University of Pennsylvania. She received her PhD from the University of Arizona in 2007. Her research focuses on the intersection of mass media and issues of diversity, such as racial stereotyping, ethnolinguistic group vitality, and ethnic identity. Kopacz's research has appeared in the *Journal of Broadcasting and Electronic Media, Electronic Journal of Communication, Human Communication Research*, and *Communication Teacher*.

LORRAINE MANGIONE, PHD, is a professor at Antioch University New England in Keene, NH (where there are very few Italians!), where she teaches doctoral students in the Department of Clinical Psychology and specializes in group therapy, supervision, and clinical training. Her dissertation explored the intersection of psychological development and the creative process; a continuing interest for her. She has published on Bruce Springsteen's music and meaning, relationships, loss, alienation, and group processes. She and her colleague, Dr. Donna DiCello, have a forthcoming book entitled *Daughters, Dads, and the Path of Grieving: Tales from Italian America* (Impact Publishing, Inc.).

RACHEL McBRIDE, PSYD, is a clinical psychologist with a private practice in Brookline, MA. She received her doctorate in clinical psychology from Antioch University New England and completed an APA approved internship at Harvard Medical School's Massachusetts Mental Health Center. McBride completed her postdoctoral training at Boston College's University Counseling Services. She is an instructor in psychology at Harvard Medical School and serves as member at large of the Massachusetts Association for Psychoanalytic Psychology. McBride is a staff consultant to an applied behavioral analysis firm in Boston and is a candidate in psychoanalytic training at Boston Psychoanalytic Society and Institute.

ANTHONY F. TASSO, PHD, earned his doctorate in clinical psychology from the University of Tennessee, and completed his doctoral internship at Pennsylvania Hospital/University of Pennsylvania. He is a New Jersey and New York licensed psychologist and is Board Certified in Clinical Psychology by the American Board of Professional Psychology (ABPP). He is the former coordinator of the Jersey Center for Non-Violence, of Jersey Battered Women's Services, Inc. (Morris County, NJ). He conducts research and clinical training in domestic violence and hypnosis. Tasso is an Associate Professor at Fairleigh Dickinson University in New Jersey and has a private practice in Morristown, NJ.

JENNIFER L. TURSI, MA, earned her master's degree in clinical mental health counseling at Fairleigh Dickinson University in New Jersey and completed her Master's internship at the Resource Center of Somerset in Hillsborough, NJ, working with survivors of domestic violence. She is a New Jersey Licensed Associate Counselor, is certified by the National Board for Certified Counselors as a National Certified Counselor, and is certified by the state of New Jersey as a Disaster Response Crisis Counselor. Tursi currently works in a school-based program which serves the mental health needs of adolescents.

Index

STUDIES IN ITALIAN AMERICANA SERIES
Published by the Calandra Institute

VOLUME 1
Uncertainty and Insecurity in the New Age
Vincent Parrillo, Editor
ISBN 978-0-9703403-4-4

VOLUME 2
Mediated Ethnicity: New Italian American Cinema
Giuliana Muscio, Joseph Sciorra, Giovanni Spagnoletti, Anthony Tamburri, Editors
ISBN 978-0-9703403-6-8

VOLUME 3
Italian American Students in New York City, 1975–2000: A Research Anthology
Nancy Ziehler, Editor
ISBN 978-0-9703403-5-1

VOLUME 4
Graces Received: Painted and Metal Ex-votos from Italy
Rosangela Briscese and Joseph Sciorra, Editors
ISBN 978-0-9703403-7-5

VOLUME 5
Italian Signs, American Politics: Current Affairs, Historical Perspectives, Empirical Analyses
Ottorino Cappelli, Editor
ISBN 978-0-9703403-8-2

VOLUME 6
New Directions in Italian American History: Selected Essays from the Conference in Honor of Philip V. Cannistraro
Ernest Ialongo and William Adams, Editors
ISBN 978-0-9703403-9-9

CPSIA information can be obtained at www.ICGtesting.com
Printed in the USA
LVOW03s1312180414

382307LV00002B/9/P